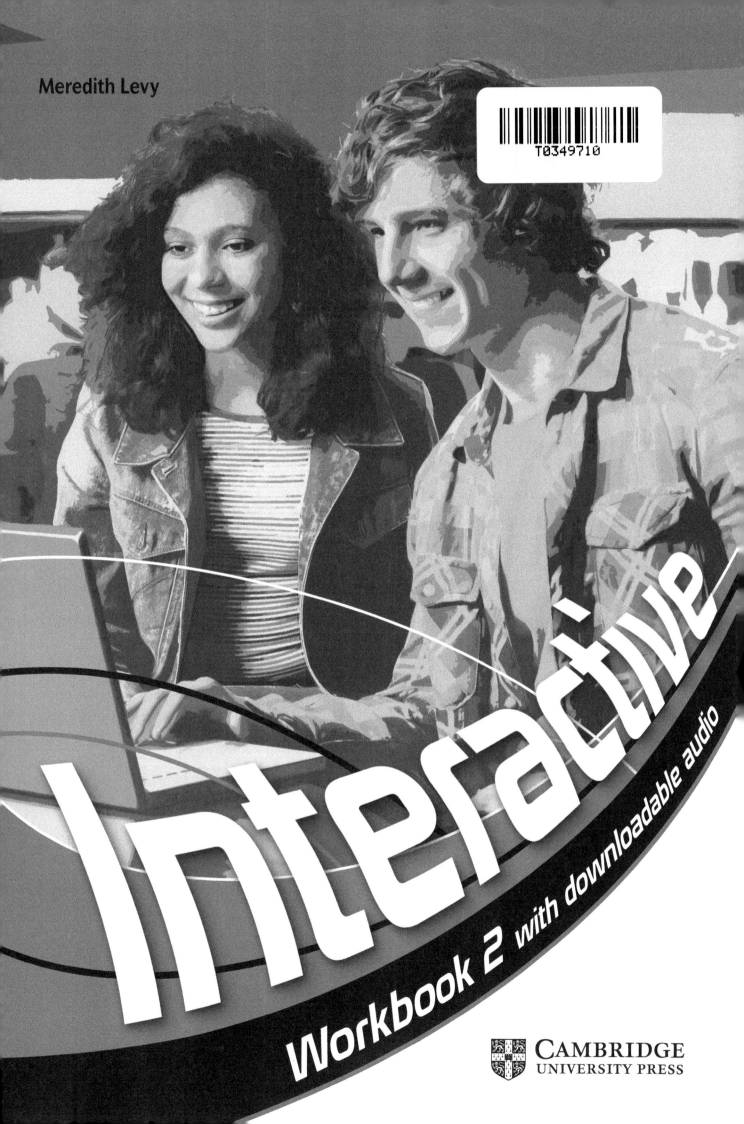

Meredith Levy

T0349710

Interactive

Workbook 2 *with downloadable audio*

CAMBRIDGE
UNIVERSITY PRESS

Shaftesbury Road, Cambridge CB2 8EA, United Kingdom

One Liberty Plaza, 20th Floor, New York, NY 10006, USA

477 Williamstown Road, Port Melbourne, VIC 3207, Australia

314–321, 3rd Floor, Plot 3, Splendor Forum, Jasola District Centre, New Delhi – 110025, India

103 Penang Road, #05-06/07, Visioncrest Commercial, Singapore 238467

Cambridge University Press & Assessment is a department of the University of Cambridge.

We share the University's mission to contribute to society through the pursuit of education, learning and research at the highest international levels of excellence.

www.cambridge.org
Information on this title: www.cambridge.org/9780521712156

© Cambridge University Press & Assessment 2011

First published 2011

20 19 18 17 16

Printed in Great Britain by CPI Group (UK) Ltd, Croydon CR0 4YY

A catalogue record for this publication is available from the British Library

ISBN 978-0-521-71215-6 Workbook with Downloadable Audio
ISBN 978-0-521-71212-5 Student's Book
ISBN 978-0-521-71216-3 Teacher's Book
ISBN 978-0-521-71217-0 Teacher's Resource Pack
ISBN 978-0-521-71218-7 Class Audio CDs
ISBN 978-0-521-14724-8 DVD (PAL)
ISBN 978-0-521-14725-5 DVD (NTSC)
ISBN 978-1-107-40212-6 Classware DVD-ROM
ISBN 978-1-107-40214-0 Testmaker CD-ROM and Audio CD

Contents

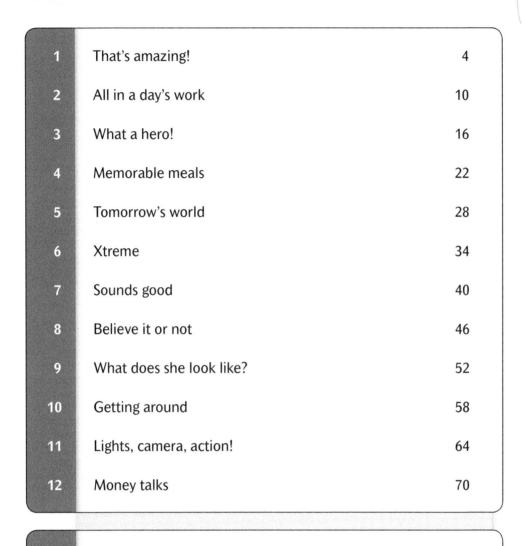

1	That's amazing!	4
2	All in a day's work	10
3	What a hero!	16
4	Memorable meals	22
5	Tomorrow's world	28
6	Xtreme	34
7	Sounds good	40
8	Believe it or not	46
9	What does she look like?	52
10	Getting around	58
11	Lights, camera, action!	64
12	Money talks	70

Grammar reference and Grammar practice	76
Irregular verbs	102
Phonemic symbols	103

1 Vocabulary

Parts of the body

a Find fourteen more parts of the body in the puzzle and write the words in the correct column.

T	O	N	G	U	E	L	R	I	C
O	H	J	E	S	A	L	X	S	H
O	P	R	U	C	N	F	B	T	I
T	O	E	O	F	K	I	R	O	N
H	A	B	V	A	L	N	A	M	W
I	H	E	A	R	T	G	I	A	R
D	O	K	N	E	E	E	N	C	I
C	H	E	S	T	G	R	E	H	S
S	H	O	U	L	D	E	R	A	T

①  ②

tongue ....

....

....

....

....

③ 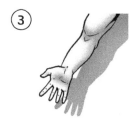 ④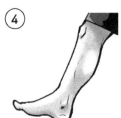

....

....

....

b Complete the sentences with the words in Exercise 1a.

1 You think with your ..brain.. .

2 Your .... is the front part of your neck.

3 Your mouth is between your nose and your ....

4 You have five ....s on each hand.

5 You have five ....s on each foot.

6 Your ....s are at the top of your arms.

7 Your .... is on the left inside your chest.

8 When you eat, the food goes to your ....

Check it out!

Don't forget these irregular plural forms:

foot → **feet** (**not** ~~foots~~)

tooth → **teeth** (**not** ~~tooths~~)

Help yourself!

Idioms with parts of the body

There are lots of English expressions with parts of the body, for example:

It **costs an arm and a leg**. (= It's very expensive.)

Can you **give me a hand**? (= Can you help me?)

Complete the sentences with the words in the box.

chest	tongue	~~chin~~	feet	tooth	fingers

1 Keep your ..chin.. up. Things will get better soon.

2 She loves cakes and desserts. She's got a sweet ....

3 Lee is having his driving test today. I've got my .... crossed for him.

4 The word is on the tip of my ...., but I just can't think of it!

5 I've got something to say to you. I really need to get it off my ....

6 Rosa was planning to sing at the concert, but now she doesn't want to do it. She's got cold ....

Start a list of idioms in your notebook.

② Grammar Grammar reference: page 76

Present simple and present continuous

a Make these sentences negative.

1 You're enjoying that pizza.

   You aren't enjoying that pizza.

2 We go to the market every weekend.

   ....

   ....

3 They're playing baseball.

   ....

   ....

4 Sofia wants to study at college next year.

   ....

   ....

5 Matheus is wearing his glasses.

   ....

   ....

6 I know the words of this song.

   ....

   ....

7 This camera costs a lot of money.

   ....

   ....

8 We're doing our homework.

   ....

   ....

b (Circle) the correct form of the verb.

1 Hurry up! *We wait / (We're waiting)* for you.

2 Mum's at home. She *doesn't work / isn't working* today.

3 Luiz *washes / is washing* his hair three times a week.

4 We *don't use / aren't using* the computer at the moment.

5 Natalia *doesn't want / isn't wanting* to come to the cinema.

6 Can you be quiet? *I try / I'm trying* to listen to the radio.

7 Luke's cousins are Canadian. *They speak / They're speaking* English and French.

8 *I don't know / I'm not knowing* how to ride a horse.

c Complete the conversations with the verbs in the present simple or the present continuous.

play	try	ring	listen	~~know~~	not hear
not answer					

Sara: I think Becky wants to come to the beach with us.

Kate: Yes, I ¹ *know* . I ² .... to call her. Her phone ³ .... but she ⁴ ....

Sara: Maybe she ⁵ .... to one of her CDs. She often ⁶ .... them so loud that she ⁷ .... the phone.

want	have	hate	sit	think	not do
not want					

Sam: Hi, Ned. How are you?

Ned: I'm OK, but it's really hot here. We ⁸ .... in front of the TV and nobody ⁹ .... to do anything. Mum ¹⁰ .... this weather and she ¹¹ .... to cook. And Pete ¹² .... his homework because he ¹³ .... his brain is too hot! Anyway, how are you?

Sam: I ¹⁴ .... a nice time in the swimming pool.

Ned: Lucky you.

③ Listen

a 🔊 1 Listen to Nicole describing photos of three people. Tick (✓) the parts of the body you hear.

arm ☐   chin ☐   ear ☐   elbow ☐   eyes ☐

fingers ☐   hand ☐   knee ☐   neck ☐

shoulder ☐   teeth ☐   tongue ☐   wrist ☐

b 🔊 1 Listen again and match the pictures with the people.

1 Nicole's mother: .....A.....   ....

2 Josie: ....

3 Antonio: ....

④ Vocabulary

The five senses

a The sense verbs are wrong in these sentences. ~~Cross out~~ the wrong verb and write the correct one.

1 Don't ~~smell~~ the wall. The paint isn't dry.

.....touch.........................

2 Listen! Can you see voices?

----

3 Touch this sauce. Does it need more salt?

----

4 It's very dark outside. I can't hear anything.

----

5 Someone is cooking fish. I can taste it.

----

b Write one example for each thing in this list. Use your own ideas.

1 something loud that you can hear

----

2 something sweet and delicious that you can taste

----

3 something cold that you can touch

----

4 something small and beautiful that you can see

----

5 something nice that you can smell

----

⑤ Pronunciation

Long and short vowel sounds

a 🔊 2 Listen to the vowel sound and write /ʊ/ or /uː/. Then listen again and repeat.

1	pull	/ʊ/	4	shoes	....
2	pool	....	5	juice	....
3	cook	....	6	good	....

b 🔊 3 Listen and write /ɑː/ or /æ/. Then listen again and repeat.

1	card	/ɑː/	4	star	....
2	cat	....	5	stand	....
3	bank	....	6	glass	....

c 🔊 4 Write these words. Then listen and repeat.

1	/hɑːd/	hard	7	/kuːl/	....
2	/hæd/	....	8	/fʊt/	....
3	/hæt/	....	9	/buːts/	....
4	/hɑːt/	....	10	/pʊt/	....
5	/klɑːs/	....	11	/gruːp/	....
6	/kæmp/	....	12	/kʊd/	....

d 🔊 **5** Listen and practise saying the phrases.

a map of the market   a hard Maths exam
a large black jacket   good fruit juice
two books and a ruler

Practise saying these words

🔊 **6** blood   delicious   elbow
exhibition   perfume   shoulder   stomach
sweet   throat   tongue   tooth   touch

---

6 Grammar Grammar reference: page 76

Present simple and present continuous: questions

a Match questions 1–6 with the answers A–F.

1 Does Alex like bananas? | E |
2 Where is your friend waiting? | |
3 When does the lesson start? | |
4 Is your brother watching TV? | |
5 Who are you texting? | |
6 How often do you have English classes? | |

A Three times a week.
B Yes, he is.
C My friend Kristina.
D At the bus stop.
E No, he doesn't.
F At 10:30.

b 🔊 **7** Complete the conversations with the verbs in the present simple or the present continuous. Then listen and check.

A: What ^{1}..are.. you ..looking... (look) at?

B: That dress.

A: ^{2}.............. you .... (like) it? It's Ellie's.

B: Wow! It's great. Where ^{3}.............. she .... (buy) her clothes?

A: She makes them herself.

A: Your neighbours are never at home! ^{4}..................
they .... (travel) at the moment?

B: Yes, they're in Spain for the summer.

A: ^{5}.............. they often .... (go)
to Spain?

B: Yes, nearly every year.

A: Where ^{6}.............. they .... (stay)
this year?

B: In Granada.

A: I can hear Ben upstairs. ^{7}.............. he
.... (do) his homework?

B: No, he's playing computer games, I think.

A: Who ^{8}.............. he .... (talk) to?

B: Our cousin Robbie. ^{9}.............. you
.... (know) him?

A: No, I don't. How often ^{10}.............. you
.... (see) him?

B: Not very often. He lives in Scotland.

c Write questions for these answers. Use your own ideas.

1 A: ....
   B: Yes, I do.

2 A: ....
   B: No, I'm not.

3 A: ....
   B: No, he isn't.

4 A: ....
   B: Every day.

5 A: ....
   B: She's studying art at college.

6 A: ....
   B: They go on Saturdays.

7 Read

a Read the text. Are the sentences *right* (✓) or *wrong* (✗)?

Nik Wallenda comes from a long line of circus performers, which goes back to the 18th century. He is the great-grandson of Karl Wallenda, who was famous for his amazing abilities on the high wire. Nik, like many other members of his family, is continuing in the family tradition. In the first photo he is walking out on the wire high over the city streets of Pittsburg, USA.

Nik now holds the world record for the highest and longest bike ride on a high wire. The second photo shows this event in October 2008, in the American city of Newark. He is riding along the wire on his bicycle. The wire is 72 metres long and it is 40 metres from the ground. There is no safety net under him.

Some people think Nik has magnets in his shoes or hidden ropes. But he doesn't wear any safety equipment at all. He is very careful, but he doesn't worry about the danger. 'I do this because I love what I do,' he says.

Nik performs on the high wire in shows all over the USA, sometimes with his wife Erendira. Their three children are now learning the skills of their famous family.

1 Karl Wallenda was Nik's grandfather. ☐

2 In the first photo Nik is performing on the high wire in Newark. ☐

3 In the second photo he is cycling on a wire that is 40 metres high. ☐

4 In these photos he is wearing special magnetic shoes. ☐

5 His life is in danger when he performs. ☐

6 Nik doesn't always perform alone. ☐

b Would you like to be one of Nik Wallenda's children? Prepare to talk about this in your next class. Make notes to help you.

....
....
....
....

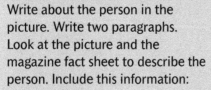

Portfolio 1

Write about the person in the picture. Write two paragraphs. Look at the picture and the magazine fact sheet to describe the person. Include this information:

Paragraph 1
- name and age
- where he lives
- what sport he does
- what he does in his free time

Paragraph 2
- what he is doing in the photo

Dylan Alcott – Paralympic athlete

Name	Dylan Alcott
Date of birth	4/12/1990
Country	Australia
Occupation	student
Sports	wheelchair basketball wheelchair tennis
Hobbies	singing, playing the drums

Quiz 1

a What do you remember about Unit 1? Answer all the questions you can and then check in the Student's Book.

A

B

C 1 2 3

1 Where does the girl in picture A come from?

....

2 What is Monsieur Mangetout doing in picture B?

....

3 Can you find six parts of the body in this puzzle?

toelbowristhroatootheart

....

....

....

4 Which two letters do you need to complete these parts of the body?

bo ☐☐   ☐☐ ck   k ☐☐ e

5 There are two mistakes in this sentence. Write the correct sentence.

I enjoy this pizza but I not wanting any ice cream.

....

....

6 ⟨Circle⟩ the correct words.

How many languages *does she speak / is she speaking*?

7 Read the question and ⟨circle⟩ the correct answer.

Are you sitting down at the moment?

A Yes, you are.   **B** Yes, I am.   **C** Yes, I do.

8 Look at picture C and write the sense verbs.

1 ....   2 ....

3 ....

9 Find three words with the sound /ɑː/ as in *car*.

start   heart   head   back   glass   care

....

10 Which word has a different vowel sound?

pull   book   could   blue

b 🔊 8 Listen and check your answers.

c Now look at your Student's Book and write three more quiz questions for Unit 1.

Question: ....
....
Answer: ....

Question: ....
....
Answer: ....

Question: ....
....
Answer: ....

All in a day's work

1 Vocabulary

Jobs

a Put the letters in order and make twelve words for jobs. Write them under the pictures.

> stinted   rusen   rifegrefith   cretathic
> ~~gerenine~~   olepic fricofe   eritaw
> sherardiser   caftroy kerrow   brumple
> justoralin   axit virred

1 ...engineer...........................

2 ....

3 ....

4 ....

5 ....

6 ....

7 ....

8 ....

9 ....

10 ....

11 ....

12 ....

b Complete the sentences with the words in Exercise 1a.

1 A ...waiter... brings you your meal in a café or restaurant.

2 If you want a new hairstyle, go to a ....

3 ....s write reports for TV or newspapers.

4 ....s design machines, roads and bridges.

5 If there's a problem with the water in your house, call a ....

6 ....s look after people in hospital.

7 If there's something wrong with your teeth, go to a ....

8 A .... stops people if they drive too fast.

9 ....s usually come quickly if a building is burning.

2 Grammar   Grammar reference: page 78

Past simple: regular and irregular verbs

a 🔊 9 Complete the texts with the verbs in the past simple. Then listen and check.

> My cousin [1] ...finished... (finish) school a year ago but he [2] .... (not go) to university. He [3] .... (work) in a shop for six months and then he [4] .... (travel) round Europe with some friends. They [5] .... (have) a really good time.

> I [6] .... (get) a job in the Plaza Café last year, but I [7] .... (hate) it. The kitchen [8] .... (not be) very clean and the food [9] .... (not taste) nice. I [10] .... (not want) to work there, so I [11] .... (leave). Two months later the café [12] .... (close).

b Complete the conversations with the verbs in the past simple.

see	~~do~~	speak	not stay	go

A: What ^{1} ..did.. you ..do.. on Saturday?

B: I ^{2} .... to the sports centre for a while. I ^{3} .... there long.

A: ^{4} .... you .... Kristina?

B: No, but I ^{5} .... to her on the phone.

be	send	buy	arrive	give	not pay

A: Owen ^{6} .... a jacket on the Internet last week.

B: ^{7} .... it expensive?

A: No, he ^{8} .... a lot, but when it ^{9} .... it was the wrong size.

B: ^{10} .... he .... it back?

A: No, he ^{11} .... it to his brother.

3 Read

What's in a name?

Before the 11th century, nobody in England had a surname. It took 400 years before people all used a surname that passed down through their family, and today's English surnames come from that time. Most of them belong to these four groups:

1 **Father's name** About 30% of English surnames came from the father's name. *Peter's son* became *Peters* or *Peterson*, *John's son* became *Johnson*, etc. The ending -*son* is like -*ez* in Spanish or -*poulos* in Greek.

2 **Place names** 40% of surnames described where someone lived. They were sometimes actual place names, but often they were natural features or buildings, for example Field, Rivers, Church, Bridge or Hall. If someone lived at the bottom of a hill or at the end of a town, they got the name Underhill or Townsend.

3 **Descriptive names** Some surnames described a type of person, for example Brown, Short, Strange, Smart or Good. Someone with white hair was called Whitehead, a tall person was Longman and someone who came from outside the village was Newman.

4 **Jobs** Some of the many English job names (like Cook, Farmer and Gardener) are easy to see – but did you know that in the past the surnames opposite were also words for jobs?

Smith: A smith was a metal worker, who often made shoes for horses.

Chandler: Chandlers made and sold candles – an important job in the days before electric lights.

Thatcher: This was a worker who made roofs for houses.

Page: A page was a young servant in a rich person's house.

To find out more about English surnames, look on the Internet!

A

B

C

D

a Look at these famous names. Match the surnames with groups 1–4 in the text.

A ☐ Michael Jackson   B ☐ Carrie Fisher

C ☐ Neil Armstrong   D ☐ Scarlett Johansson

E ☐ Will Young   F ☐ Elijah Wood

G ☐ Justin Timberlake   H ☐ Minnie Driver

b Match the jobs with the pictures above.

smith *picture* ......   chandler *picture* ......

thatcher *picture* ......   page *picture* ......

c What do you know about your surname? Are there surnames in your country that belong to groups 1–4 in the text? Prepare to talk about this in your next lesson. Make notes to help you.

....

....

....

....

....

4 Vocabulary

Verb/noun collocations

a (Circle) the correct verb.

1 Police officers usually *do / wear* a uniform.

2 'Who can *take / answer* the question?' asked the teacher.

3 We usually *do / make* our homework after dinner.

4 They *start / do* work at 8:30am.

5 Mum *made / took* lunch for ten people on Saturday.

6 This is difficult. Can you *answer / help* me with it?

b Complete the sentences. Use words from each box.

make	take	do

a phone call	a mistake
the shopping	friends
your bed	~~some photos~~
sport	

1 I'd like to ~~take some photos~~ but I haven't got my camera here.

2 We .... in our PE classes at school.

3 Ben followed the instructions very carefully. He didn't want to ....

4 Where's my phone? I need to ....
....

5 Mum and Dad usually .... at our local supermarket.

6 Everyone likes Omar and Ayesha. They ....
.... easily.

7 Please tidy your room and ....
....

Help yourself!

More collocations with *make* and *take*

Guess the correct verb, *make* or *take*, in these sentences. Then check in your dictionary.

1 We need to .... **plans** for our holiday in August.

2 We've worked for three hours. It's time to .... **a break**.

3 Shh! Don't .... **a noise** when you come in.

4 You can .... **money** in this job if you work hard.

5 .... this **medicine** three times a day.

6 Let's .... **a walk** along the beach.

7 It's OK, you don't need to hurry. ....
your time!

8 .... **a list** of the things you need.

In your notebook, list all the collocations you know with *make* and *take*. Add example sentences so you can see how the expressions are used.

(5) Pronunciation

Silent consonants

a 🔊 10 Listen to the word pairs. Tick (✓) the word with the silent consonant. Then listen again and repeat.

1	climber	✓	number	☐
2	milk	☐	walk	☐
3	listened	☐	listed	☐
4	children	☐	chemist	☐
5	science	☐	Scotland	☐
6	shelf	☐	half	☐
7	two	☐	twenty	☐
8	after	☐	often	☐

b 🔊 11 (Circle) the silent consonant in each word. Then listen, check and repeat.

could   cupboard   foreign   autumn
orchestra   island

c 🔊 12 Listen and tick (✓) the words where you hear the consonant /g/. Then listen again and repeat.

long ☐   longer ☐   finger ☐   singer ☐
hungry ☐   design ☐   tongue ☐

Practise saying these words

🔊 13 accident   architect   dangerous
factory   hairdresser   journalist   nurse
poor   uniform

---

(6) Grammar Grammar reference: page 78

used to

a Look at the photo from 1890 and complete the sentences with *used to* or *didn't use to* and the correct verb.

| travel | ~~wear~~ | pull | wear | have | make |

1 Men and women ..used to wear.. hats.
2 Women .... short skirts.
3 People .... by car.
4 Horses .... buses along the street.
5 Nobody .... phone calls.
6 Streets and shops .... electric lights.

b There is a mistake in each of these sentences. ~~Cross out~~ the wrong word(s) and write the correct word(s).

1 I used to ~~loved~~ climbing trees. ..love..
2 My grandmother use to work as a journalist.
....
3 When Dad was young, he uses sing in a rock band. ....
4 Danielle used to take that photo in 2007.
....
5 Most people don't use to travel far in the 19th century. ....
6 100 years ago people not used to have televisions. ....
7 Were you use to play with toy cars?
....
8 Did your sister used to go to this school?
....

7 Listen

◁)) 14 Listen to the five recordings. Tick (✓) the correct answer: A, B or C.

1 What is his job?

A ☐　　　　B ☐　　　　C ☐

2 What was his father's first job?

A ☐　　　　B ☐　　　　C ☐

3 Which hairstyle does Emma have now?

A ☐　　　　B ☐　　　　C ☐

4 What used to grow in her great-grandmother's garden?

A ☐　　　　B ☐　　　　C ☐

5 What did he use in his recipe?

A ☐　　　　B ☐　　　　C ☐

Portfolio 2

Write about yourself when you were a child. Write two paragraphs.

Paragraph 1
Describe what you used to do and enjoy. Think about some of these things:

- games
- music
- TV shows
- food
- friends
- your first school

Paragraph 2
Describe one interesting thing that happened. Start with a time expression.

One day …
In 2006 …
When I was five …
When I first went to school …

If you want to, find a photo to go with your description.

Check it out!

Remember, *used to* is for activities that happened often or normally in the past. For a particular action or event, use the past simple.

I **used to wear** a Batman costume.
I **wore** it for the first time on my sixth birthday.

Quiz 2

a What do you remember about Unit 2? Answer all the questions you can and then check in the Student's Book.

A

B

ON THE THAMES AT LOW WATER.

1 What is the job in picture A?

....

2 Circle the odd one out.

plumber   nurse   dentist   doctor

3 Which job is the most dangerous?

architect   firefighter   waiter

4 Circle the correct word.

She works *to* / *at* / *as* a police officer.

5 Where did the children in picture B live and work? Name the city.

....

6 Write these verbs in the past simple.

stand ....

grow ....

lose ....

7 Read the answer and complete the question.

A: .... Diana?

B: I saw her at the market.

8 Which verb (*make*, *take* or *do*) do you need to find a way through this puzzle?

→

dinner	a question	sport
my bed	friends	the shopping
a photo	lunch	a phone call
a friend	school	a mistake

→

Verb: ....

9 There are two mistakes in this sentence. Write the correct sentence.

Tom use live in Berlin, but in 2007 he use to move to Paris.

....

....

10 Which word starts with a silent *h*?

hot   hour   hotel   holiday

b 🔊 15 Listen and check your answers.

c Now look at your Student's Book and write three more quiz questions for Unit 2.

Question: ....

....

Answer: ....

Question: ....

....

Answer: ....

Question: ....

....

Answer: ....

3) What a hero!

(1) Vocabulary

-ed and -ing adjectives

a (Circle) the correct adjective.

1 My phone rang in the middle of the film and everyone looked at me. I was *embarrassed / disappointed*.

2 My little brother is *frightened / excited* because it's his birthday tomorrow.

3 I think you'll enjoy these magazines. They're *interesting / surprising*.

4 A tree fell in the storm and hit the back of the house. It was a *frightening / boring* experience.

5 Marco didn't do well in his exams and he was very *interested / disappointed*.

6 We were *surprised / bored* when Gabriela arrived! We thought she was in Barcelona.

b Complete the adjectives with the correct ending.

Phil and Lily went to the football on Saturday, but the match wasn't very ¹excit_ing____ . Lily was ²disappoint_____ because her team didn't win. Phil wasn't ³interest_____ in the match. He thought it was ⁴bor_____ .

When I saw the spider, I was ⁵frighten_____ and I jumped onto a chair. The others were ⁶surpris_____ and they thought I was stupid. It was very ⁷embarrass_____ .

> ### Check it out!
>
> **Here are some more -ed/-ing adjectives:**
>
> tired – tiring   worried – worrying
> amazed – amazing   terrified – terrifying

> ### Help yourself!
>
> **Compound nouns with -ing words**
> *Swimming* pool and *dining* room are examples of compound nouns with *-ing* words.
>
> Look at the pictures and complete the compound nouns. Use the *-ing* form of these verbs.
>
> | wash | fly | live | sleep | ~~walk~~ | race |
> |------|-----|------|-------|----------|------|
>
>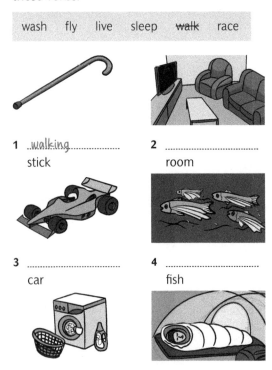
>
> 1 ..walking.............   2 ....
>   stick   room
>
> 3 ....   4 ....
>   car   fish
>
> 5 ....   6 ....
>   machine   bag
>
> Find some compound nouns with these *-ing* verbs. Use your dictionary.
>
> driving   shopping   reading
>
> List the compound nouns in your notebook.

(2) **Grammar** Grammar reference: page 80

Past continuous

a Complete the sentences with the correct form of the verb *be*.

1 I saw your neighbours at the supermarket. They ...were... doing the shopping.
2 At 8 o'clock this morning I .... sitting in the train.
3 I remember it was a warm evening, so you .... wearing a coat.
4 Sara wasn't at the swimming pool. She .... working all weekend.
5 There was nobody at home on Saturday. We .... visiting my uncle.
6 Tony didn't come to school yesterday because he .... feeling well.

b What was happening at 11 o'clock? Choose words from both boxes and use the verbs in the past continuous.

| clean | stand | drink | ~~ride~~ | take | talk | | coffee | photos | windows | at the bus stop |
| | | | | | | | ~~her bike~~ | on the phone | | |

1 Sophie ...was riding her bike. ....
2 Pavel and Yasmin ....
3 Nuria ....
4 Tim and Daniel ....
5 Martin ....
6 Three people ....

c Write the questions and then write the answers.

1 Sophie / wear / a jacket?
  A: ...Was Sophie wearing a jacket? ....
  B: ...Yes, she was. ....

2 Martin / sit down?
  A: ....
  B: ....

3 Pavel and Yasmin / eat?
  A: ....
  B: ....

4 Nuria's phone / ring?
  A: ....
  B: ....

5 Tim and Daniel / work / hard?
  A: ....
  ....
  B: ....

③ Listen

a 🔊 **16** Listen. What happened yesterday? Tick (✓) the correct picture.

Ⓐ

☐

Ⓑ

☐

Ⓒ

☐

b 🔊 **16** Listen again and (circle) the correct words.

1 Greg was *inside / outside* when the storm started.
2 He was *working on his computer / listening to music*.
3 He was sitting in the dark *when he heard a loud noise / while the rain was falling*.
4 Lisa and her father were driving *slowly / quickly* through the forest.
5 The tree *hit / didn't hit* the car.
6 Lisa felt *sad / frightened* during the storm.
7 Greg felt *worried / excited*.

④ Vocabulary

Ages and stages

a Use the letters *a*, *d*, *e* and *t* to complete these words. Then write the words in the lists.

1 b <u>a</u> by
2 chil _
3 _ l _ _ rly
4 _ _ _ n _ g _ r
5 mi _ _ l _ - _ g _ _
6 _ o _ _ l _ r

Nouns	Adjectives
..baby..............	....
....	....
....	
....	

b Complete the sentences.

①

She's a ..baby... .

②

I'm 45.

He's a .... person.
He's in his ....-forties.

③

I'm 78.

He's an .... person.
He's in his .... seventies.

④

I'm 3.

She's a ....

⑤

I'm 22.

He's in his .... twenties.

⑥

I'm 17.

She's a ....

⑤ Grammar Grammar reference: page 80

Past simple and past continuous

> **Check it out!**
>
> **We can change the order of the two actions.**
>
> While _Maria was watching TV_, the phone rang.
>
> _Maria was watching TV_ when the phone rang.
>
> When the phone rang, _Maria was watching TV_.
>
> The phone rang while _Maria was watching TV_.

a Complete the sentences with *when* or *while*.

1 .... Pavel was coming home, he heard someone call for help.

2 They were driving down Johnson Street .... the accident happened.

3 .... we were sitting in the garden, a fire started in the kitchen.

4 I broke my wrist .... I was surfing at Blackwater Beach.

5 Nadia was waiting at the door .... the police arrived.

6 .... you rang me, I was running to catch the bus.

b Complete the sentences with the correct form of the verbs.

play	~~meet~~	fly	fall over	find	leave
have	cycle	~~shop~~	drop	rain	clean

1 I ..was shopping.. at the market when I ..met.. Josef.

4 It .... when the girls .... the museum.

⑥ Pronunciation

Intonation and emotions

a 🔊 **17** Listen. The speaker says each sentence twice. Write 1 or 2 for each emotion, A and B. Then listen again and repeat.

1 I watched that film last night.

  A [2] disappointed   B [1] excited

2 No, I don't want to go out.

  A [ ] frightened   B [ ] angry

3 I'm doing my History project.

  A [ ] interested   B [ ] bored

4 Oh! I didn't know you were here.

  A [ ] surprised   B [ ] embarrassed

b 🔊 **18** Listen and tick (✓) the sentences where you hear strong emotion. Then listen again and repeat.

1 Thanks a lot for your help. [ ]

2 Look, it's raining again. [ ]

3 There's a crocodile in the river. [ ]

4 They've got over 500 CDs. [ ]

5 Be careful – that's dangerous. [ ]

> **Practise saying these words**
>
> 🔊 **19** angry   attack   breathe disappointed   embarrassing   exciting frightened   interesting   middle-aged realise   surprised   toddler

2 Marina .... while she .... hockey.

5 A bird .... into the room while we .... lunch.

3 While Dan .... the car, he .... my earring.

6 While Sam .... to school, he .... his folders.

(7) Read

a Read the article. Which two pictures show what happened in these stories?

 1 ☐
 2 ☐
 3 ☐
 4 ☐

Two teenagers received the Carnegie Medal for acts of heroism yesterday

Tom Foust, 17, saved the life of an 83-year-old woman while he was driving home in Glenview on 10th September. At a railway crossing Mrs Ida Kurtz drove onto the railway line, where her car got stuck. At the same time, two trains were racing towards the crossing from different directions. Tom ran to the woman's car. He opened the door, unclipped the safety belt and pulled her outside. Then he covered her with his body as the first train hit the car at 125 kph. Seconds later, the second train also hit the car. 'It was like a scene from a movie,' Tom said later. Mrs Kurtz was very frightened but she was not hurt.

Chloe Van Alstine, also 17, was going for a run near Lake Algonquin in the state of New York when she heard a loud noise and saw a lorry go off the road and into the lake. The driver, William Trainor, 48, got out through the window but, as Chloe said later, 'the water was so cold he couldn't move – he just kept going under'. Chloe ran across the bridge and into the water. She grabbed Mr Trainor's arms, pulled his head out of the water and started swimming back with him. On the way, a man met them in a boat and helped them to safety.

b Choose the correct answer: A, B or C.

1 Tom and Chloe got prizes because
  A they were teenagers.
  B they were heroes.
  C they both saved the life of an elderly person.

2 Mrs Kurtz was in danger because
  A two trains were coming towards her.
  B she couldn't stop her car.
  C she couldn't open the car door.

3 When Tom got to Mrs Kurtz, she
  A was getting out of the car.
  B was standing near the car.
  C was sitting inside the car.

4 Chloe saw the accident while she was
  A swimming.
  B running.
  C going across the bridge.

5 When Chloe reached Mr Trainor, he
  A wasn't breathing.
  B wasn't able to swim.
  C couldn't escape from the lorry.

6 Chloe was swimming back with Mr Trainor when
  A she grabbed his arms.
  B he went under the water.
  C a boat arrived.

Portfolio 3

Write about an important or unusual event that happened to you (or to someone you know). Write two paragraphs. For example:
• when you first met someone
• when you got some good news
• when an accident happened
• when you escaped from danger.

Paragraph 1
• When did the event happen?
• Where were you and what were you doing?
• What were other people doing?

Paragraph 2
• What happened?

Quiz 3

a What do you remember about Unit 3? Answer all the questions you can and then check in the Student's Book.

A

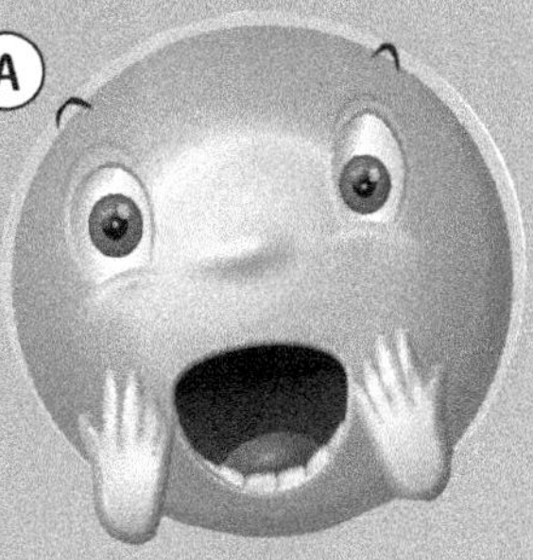

B

PRESS START

C

1 What is the adjective for the feeling in picture A?

....

2 Complete the adjectives.

Everyone was excit.......... before the concert, but it was very disappoint.......... .

3 (Circle) the odd one out.

boring   embarrassing   breathing   frightening

4 Complete the missing word.

V _ _ _ _ _ _ _ _s are people who work because they want to. They don't get any money for their work.

5 An animal attacked Juliet Peters in Australia. What was it?

....

6 Look at picture B. What were the girls doing at nine o' clock last night?

....

....

7 Correct the spelling of the *-ing* forms.

takeing ....   siting ....

happenning ....

8 Choose the correct ending.

The fire started while we ...
A were sleeping.   **B** woke up.
C called the fire service.

9 Look at picture C and complete the sentence.

While Stefan .... a shower, his phone ....

10 Put these words in order (1–5), from youngest to oldest.

teenager ☐   elderly person ☐
child ☐   baby ☐   toddler ☐

b 🔊 20 Listen and check your answers.

c Now look at your Student's Book and write three more quiz questions for Unit 3.

Question: ....
....
Answer: ....

Question: ....
....
Answer: ....

Question: ....
....
Answer: ....

1 Vocabulary

Adjectives

a Put the boxes in order and make eight adjectives.

xuri	licio	mazi	~~dy de~~	ird lu
mora	gust	razy a	ous me	
~~tren~~	ble c	ng dis	us we	ing

trendy ....
de ....
....
....

b Write the adjectives from Exercise 1a.

1 a ....
ice cream

2 a ....
hairstyle

3 a ....
dog

4 a ....
hotel

5 ....
food

6 an ....
computer game

7 ....
clothes

8 a ....
experience

2 Grammar Grammar reference: page 82

Comparative and superlative adjectives

a 🔊 21 (Circle) the correct words. Then listen and check.

A: The Grand Hotel is the ¹more luxurious / (most luxurious) hotel in town.
B: Well, it's definitely the ²more expensive / most expensive hotel. But lots of people say the Carlton is ³friendlier / friendliest and ⁴more comfortable / most comfortable than the Grand.

A: Which subject is ⁵easier / easiest for you, History or Geography?
B: I think History is ⁶harder / hardest, but it's also ⁷more interesting / most interesting than Geography. Actually, Science is the ⁸more difficult / most difficult subject at school for me.

A: Look at these! They're the ⁹more terrible / most terrible photos I've ever taken.
B: You probably need a ¹⁰better / best camera.
A: No, the camera's OK. It's just that I'm the world's ¹¹worse / worst photographer.

b Write sentences with the comparative or superlative form of the adjectives.

short   bad   expensive   ~~big~~   angry
tall   modern   ~~happy~~

1 Russia / country
   Russia is the biggest country.

2 Alex / Daniel
   Alex is happier than Daniel.

3 Pietro / student
   ....

4 Emma / Julie
   ....

5 the jacket / the skirt
   ....
   ....

6 February / month
   ....
   ....

7 Claire's Boutique / shop
   ....
   ....

8 the pizza / the pasta
   ....
   ....

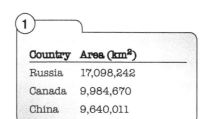

Country	Area (km²)
Russia	17,098,242
Canada	9,984,670
China	9,640,011

Alex and Daniel

Pietro

Emma and Julie

$120 $65

FEBRUARY

pound sense   CLAIRE'S BOUTIQUE   grocery

Mine's bad   Very bad

c Complete the sentences so they are true for you. Use the comparative or superlative form of the adjectives.

1 *My father* is *taller* (tall) than me.

2 For me, the .... (bad) day of the week is ....

3 My .... is my .... (important) possession.

4 .... is a .... (good) singer than me.

5 .... is the .... (interesting) programme on TV at the moment.

6 .... is the .... (funny) person I know.

7 I think .... is a .... (exciting) film than ....

8 In my country, ... is a .... (hot) month than ....

Help yourself!

Common adjective endings (1)

Here are three typical endings for adjectives.

-y   trend**y**
-al   fin**al**
-ful   wonder**ful**

Complete these adjectives with the correct ending and write them in the lists below.

aw...............   norm...............   craz...............

tast...............   care...............   digit...............

use...............   angr...............   ide...............

-y	**-al**	**-ful**
trendy	*final*	*wonderful*
....	....	....
....	....	....
....	....	....

Can you think of other adjectives to add? Write the lists in your notebook.

3 Read

a Read the text and match the paragraphs (1–3) with the photos.

1 The world's largest restaurant is the Damascus Gate. Located in the Syrian capital, Damascus, it has seats for 6,014 customers. The dining area is 54,000 m², divided into different areas. In the busiest months of the year, up to 1,800 people work in the restaurant, and the kitchens can produce a dish every two seconds. They serve Chinese and Indian food as well as Middle Eastern dishes.

2 In New York's Serendipity 3 restaurant, you can order the most expensive ice cream dessert in the world. The ingredients include the best vanilla from Madagascar, one of the world's most luxurious types of chocolate from Venezuela and special sugary fruits from Paris. It is covered with thin leaves of real gold, which you can eat, and there is a golden sugar flower on top. The price? $1,000!

3 An Indian woman, Anandita Dutta Tamuly, broke a world record when she ate a plate of the world's hottest chillies. The *bhut jolokia* chilli is so strong that the smallest piece creates an extreme burning feeling in the mouth that lasts for hours. Anandita ate 51 of these chillies in two minutes. The earlier record-holder was a South African who ate a total of eight 'normal' chillies in one minute.

b Are the sentences *right* (✓) or *wrong* (✗) or *doesn't say* (−)?

1 The Damascus Gate is bigger than any other restaurant. ☐

2 There are always 1,800 workers at the Damascus Gate. ☐

3 A meal is cheaper at the Damascus Gate than at the Serendipity 3. ☐

4 The Serendipity 3 uses very special ingredients for its ice cream dessert. ☐

5 This dessert is one of the most popular dishes in New York. ☐

6 Anandita Dutta Tamuly enjoys eating chillies. ☐

7 *Bhut jolokia* chillies are more difficult to eat than 'normal' chillies. ☐

8 Anandita is the first person to have a world record for eating chillies. ☐

4 Grammar Grammar reference: page 82

Modifiers

a There is a mistake in each of these sentences. ~~Cross out~~ the wrong word(s) and write the correct word(s).

1 It's ~~the~~ lot warmer today than yesterday.

....a...............................

2 This is much a better computer than my old one.

....

3 They're both good phones, but this one is a bit most expensive.

....

4 Mr and Mrs Hill are lot friendly than our other neighbours.

....

5 Our team was more much successful last year.

....

6 The café is always a bit noisiest than the restaurant upstairs.

....

Check it out!

We use *a lot* and *much* only with comparative adjectives.

With the base form of the adjective, we can use *really*, *very* or *extremely*.

I'm **really** hungry. (**not** ~~a lot hungry~~ or ~~much hungry~~)

They're a **very** famous band.

It was **extremely** cold last night.

b (Circle) the correct words.

1 They've painted the café in *much / very* nicer colours.

2 The meal was *a lot / really* delicious.

3 Kate looks a lot *pretty / prettier* with short hair.

4 The shops here are much *busy / busier* in the summer.

5 The food at this restaurant used to be *a lot / very* better.

6 I ordered a chicken salad. The other dishes were *much / much more* expensive.

7 Don't touch this plate. It's *a lot / very* hot.

8 We all thought the exam was *much / really* difficult.

5 Vocabulary

Eating out

a Make seven words for things you see on a dining table. Use one letter from each column.

¹G	L	A	S	S		²P			
				³					
⁴						⁵			
⁶									
			⁷						

```
            S    L  I
      F  E       R  O  T
  G   N  B   S   F  P  S  L  O  H
  K   A  A   N   E  O  P  K  N  T  N
  T   L  I   L   A  C  K  P  A  O  E
```

b Write the words.

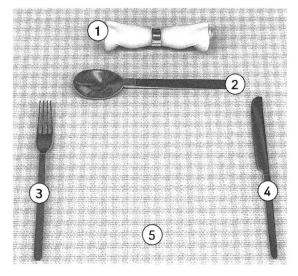

1 .... 4 ....

2 .... 5 ....

3 ....

6 .... 7 ....

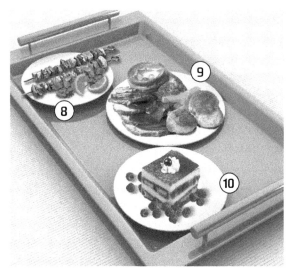

8 .... 10 ....

9 ....

c Complete the sentences with the words in Exercises 5a and 5b.

1 You put your food on a .... and take it to the table.

2 When people cut the meat on their plate, they normally use a .... in their right hand and a .... in their left hand.

3 When we have a cold drink, we normally put it in a ....

4 If you need to clean your mouth or your fingers, use your ....

5 You use a small .... to put sugar in your coffee.

6 The .... comes before the main course and the .... comes at the end of the meal.

6 Pronunciation

Word stress

a 🔊 22 Listen and underline the stressed syllable. Then listen again and repeat.

2 syllables	3 syllables
<u>cra</u>|zy	dis|gus|ting
a|mazed	ro|man|tic
nor|mal	sen|si|tive
co|rrect	el|der|ly

b 🔊 23 Write these words on the correct line to show the stress. Then listen, check and repeat.

~~napkin~~   delicious   dessert
cutlery   waiter   exciting
surprised   comfortable

1 ●•   ..napkin..   ....
2 •●   ....
3 ●••   ....
4 •●•   ....

c 🔊 24 Listen and practise saying the phrases.

a trendy café   a dirty tablecloth
tropical fish   an incredible experience
a delicious dinner

7 Listen

🔊 26 Listen to Adam and Lara talking about the Seaview restaurant. Complete the table. Write ✓ for a positive opinion and ✗ for a negative opinion.

	Appearance (does it look nice?)	Food	Service from the waiters	Price
Adam	....	....	....	....
Lara	....	....	....	....

Portfolio 4

Describe a restaurant or café that you know.

- Where is it and when is it open?
- What does it look like? (size? colours? decoration?)
- What sort of food can you get there? Is it good? Is it expensive?
- What is the best thing on the menu?

Quiz (4)

a What do you remember about Unit 4? Answer all the questions you can and then check in the Student's Book.

A

B

C

(1) Where is the restaurant in picture A?

....

(2) What is unusual about the waiters at Dans le Noir restaurant?

....

(3) Add vowels (a, e, i, o, u) to make three adjectives.

mzng .... mmrbl ....

dlcs ....

(4) Which adjective describes the costume in picture B? Tick (✓) one.

weird ☐ luxurious ☐ trendy ☐

(5) Circle the correct words.

This duck is the *nicer / nicest* dish on the menu. It's *tastier / tastiest* than the fish.

(6) Complete the sentences with the correct form of the adjectives.

I've read the book, but the film is much .... (interesting). In fact, it's the .... (good) film I've seen.

(7) One word is wrong in each sentence. ~~Cross it out~~ and write the correct word.

a You clean your mouth with a tablecloth.

....

b You drink water from a bowl.

....

c The main course comes after the dessert.

....

(8) What is missing from the restaurant table in picture C?

....

(9) Choose the correct answer: A, B or C.

The new cinema is .... comfortable than the old one.

A the more **B** a lot more **C** the much more

(10) Underline the stress in these words.

crazy disgusting memorable

b 🔊 27 Listen and check your answers.

c Now look at your Student's Book and write three more quiz questions for Unit 4.

Question: ....

....

Answer: ....

Question: ....

....

Answer: ....

Question: ....

....

Answer: ....

5 Tomorrow's world

1 Vocabulary

Transport

a Write words 1–8 in the puzzle. Then put the ◯ letters in the right order to make one more transport word.

1 T R A M
2
3
4
5
6
7
8

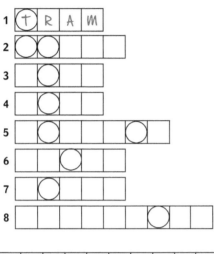

b Complete the sentences with the words in Exercise 1a.

1 My uncle uses his .... for fishing.

2 A .... can come down on the top of a building.

3 Two people can ride on a .... It's a powerful machine.

4 A .... is different from a bus because it travels along the road on rails.

5 A .... is slower than a motorbike and it's a lot cheaper.

6 100 years ago, people travelled from Europe to the USA by ....

7 Over 500 people can fly on a modern ....

8 You can take your car from England to France on a ....

9 Kevin drives a .... for one of the big supermarkets.

Help yourself!

UK and US English

Sometimes there are differences between UK English and US English words.

lorry (UK English) = *truck* (US English)

aeroplane (UK English) = *airplane* (US English)

Match these words and write them in the lists. Use your dictionary if you need to.

chips   soccer   holiday   trousers   cinema   football
vacation   pants   French fries   movie theater

UK	USA
lorry	truck
aeroplane	airplane
....	....
....	....
....	....
....	....
....	....

Look up the word *autumn* in your dictionary. Can you find the US English word? ....

Then look up *cookie*. Can you find the UK English word? ....

② Grammar Grammar reference: page 84

Future predictions: *might/will*

a Circle the correct words.

1 I think *we have / we'll have* much faster computers in the future.

2 These questions are difficult, so you *might / might not* know all the answers.

3 I'm sure it *won't / might not* rain tonight. There isn't a cloud in the sky.

4 *Will people / People will they* drive electric cars in the future?

5 *We'll / We might* go swimming tomorrow, but I'm not sure about that.

6 Eva never eats meat, so she *won't / might not* order steak.

7 What presents *you'll get / will you get* for your birthday next week?

8 I'll certainly try to help you, but I *won't / might not* have time.

b 🔊 28 Complete the conversations with *will/'ll*, *won't*, *might* or *might not*. Then listen and check.

Adam: Do you want to go shopping tomorrow? We ¹ _might_ find some good shoes. The shoe shop is closing, and the sign in the window says everything ² _____ be half price.

Marco: That sounds good, but I ³ _____ be able to go. It depends on Mum. She ⁴ _____ want me to help with the painting.

Adam: That ⁵ _____ take long! You can do it this afternoon.

Marco: Yes, we've started, but we ⁶ _____ finish today. No way!

Marina: ⁷ _____ Tony and Andrea be here before eight o'clock?

Alice: Yes, they ⁸ _____ . They're coming on the 7:30 bus.

Marina: I'm worried about the music. Tony ⁹ _____ remember to bring his CDs. I hope that won't happen, but he's got a bad memory.

Alice: No, it's OK – he ¹⁰ _____ forget. I rang him an hour ago. Where are you going to put the CD player?

Marina: I'm not sure. I ¹¹ _____ put it on the piano. What do you think?

Alice: Yes, good idea. I think it ¹² _____ be OK there.

c Write sentences with *will*, *won't*, *might* or *might not*.

1 We haven't made any definite plans for the weekend. *We / go / skiing*

   We might go skiing.

2 *Carla / give / me a present* She doesn't know it's my birthday.

   _____

3 *Steve / want / to watch the tennis* He hates it.

   _____

4 I don't know if I can come to the concert. *I / have / enough money*

   _____

5 Put the knives and forks on the table, please. *Dinner / be / ready in five minutes*

   _____

6 It's a fantastic film! *You / love / it*

   _____

7 Why don't you look for your glasses in the garden? *They / be / there*

   _____

8 I'm a bit worried about my Science exam. *I / pass*

   _____

③ Read

http://www.have-your-say.net/news/future_cars

A design team has created this design for the car of the future. Nobody will drive it. You'll tell the car where to go and it will take you there, using computer technology. You can call the car to come and meet you, and after you get out, it will find a parking space. It will run on electricity, with motors in the wheels. Seven passengers will be able to sit in a comfortable space like a small living room. They'll be able to chat, watch films, make phone calls, work, sleep or just enjoy the ride. This car is only an idea at the moment, but the designers say it might be on our roads by 2040.

Posted by Claude at 4:25 PM November 17

Comments

RebeccaW
Wow! I can't wait to ride in one of these!

rickb
Forget it. We'll never see this car on the road. The idea is totally unrealistic.

dodo
Self-drive cars might be good for some people, but I like driving, so I won't buy one.

Laserman
This is the way forward. Over 90% of accidents happen because of people's mistakes. This type of car will hardly ever have an accident because it won't depend on a human driver.

Chloe
The perfect computer is just a dream. They crash, they go wrong, they do weird things. If computers drive cars, more people might die on the roads.

flik
Think about it, Chloe. Sensitive computers will be much safer than bad drivers or people who fall asleep while they're driving.

a Read Claude's blog about a design for a car. Answer the questions *Yes* or *No*.

1 Will the car need a driver? ....
2 Will the car use petrol? ....
3 Will the car be able to move if there aren't any people inside? ....
4 Will passengers be able to relax during their trip? ....
5 Can you buy this car now? ....

b Read the six Comments in the blog. Complete the sentences with the correct names.

1 .... isn't interested in getting a self-drive car.
2 .... thinks self-drive cars might be dangerous.
3 .... is excited about the car.
4 .... and .... think this type of car will be safer than the cars we have now.
5 .... doesn't believe it will be possible to make this car.

c What do you think of the design? Prepare to talk about this in your next class. Make notes to help you.

....
....
....
....
....
....
....

④ Pronunciation

Consonant clusters

a 🔊 29 Listen and tick (✓) the word you hear.

1	try	☐	tie	☐
2	quick	☐	kick	☐
3	playing	☐	paying	☐
4	score	☐	saw	☐
5	quarter	☐	water	☐
6	plan	☐	pan	☐
7	training	☐	raining	☐
8	skirt	☐	shirt	☐

b 🔊 **30** Listen and write the missing consonants. Then listen again and repeat.

1 t r am   5 _ _ ip
2 _ _ in   6 _ _ _ ong
3 _ _ ate   7 _ _ _ ing
4 _ _ ice   8 _ _ _ een

c 🔊 **31** Listen and practise saying the sentences.

1 That's a pretty skirt.
2 The queen is staying in Scotland.
3 Clare scored a quick goal.
4 Plant your strawberries in the spring.

Practise saying these words

🔊 **32** aeroplane automatic course driver engine human keyboard mechanic motorbike scooter search

---

5 Grammar Grammar reference: page 86

going to for future plans

a Look at the picture and correct the sentences. Use *going to*.

1 Jack is going to wash the lorry.

He isn't going to wash the lorry. He's going to drive the lorry.

2 Jess and Luis are going to walk to school.

....
....

3 Marta is going to drive her car.

....
....

4 The women are going to go swimming.

....
....

b Write the questions with *going to* and complete the answers.

1 you / ring / your parents?

Are you going to ring your parents?

Yes, *I am* .

2 Anna / come / with us?

....

No, ...

3 the players / start / training next week?

....

Yes, ...

4 you / order / a dessert?

....

No, ...

5 your uncle / travel / by plane?

....

Yes, ...

6 Vocabulary

Computers

a Use letters from the three boxes to make seven computer words. Write them under the pictures.

se	pri		ea	pt		ard	op
sp	m		bo	re		en	am
key	we		bc	ou		kers	er
la			nt			se	

1 .... 5 *screen*
2 .... 6 ....
3 .... 7 ....
4 ....

b Complete the sentences.

1 To watch a film on your computer, first put the DVD into the disk ....

2 A USB .... is a place where you can connect a camera to your computer.

3 A .... stick makes it easy to move files from one computer to another.

c ~~Cross out~~ the wrong word in each sentence. Write the correct word.

1 When you save your ~~fire~~, you need to give it a name.   *file* ....

2 When you kick on 'SEND', the computer will send your email.   ....

3 Google is an example of a search expert.   ....

4 When you cut and place, you move something to a different part of your document.   ....

5 Facebook is an example of a special networking site.   ....

6 ◀ This is an example of an onion.   ....

⑦ Listen

🔊 **33** Listen to the five conversations. Tick (✓) the correct answer: A, B or C.

1 How will they arrive in Greece?

A ☐   B ☐   C ☐

4 Which part of the computer has a problem?

A ☐   B ☐   C ☐

2 What does Jill predict for tomorrow morning?

A ☐   B ☐   C ☐

5 Which prediction does Matt feel sure about?

A ☐   B ☐   C ☐

3 Where is Nicola now?

A ☐   B ☐   C ☐

Portfolio 5

Write about your own life in the future. Write two paragraphs.

1 Plans for the immediate future
What are you going to do in the next few years?
- studies?
- sports and hobbies?

2 Predictions for later
What will/might you do when you are older?
- job?
- travel?
- marriage, children?

Quiz 5

a What do you remember about Unit 5? Answer all the questions you can and then check in the Student's Book.

A

B

TEMFA
Y O R L P

1 Which three types of transport can you see in picture A?

....

....

C

2 Can you find three types of transport in the puzzle in B? Each word contains the letter R.

....

6 Tick the things you can see in picture C.

laptop ☐   speakers ☐   printer ☐

webcam ☐

3 Which form of transport travels on the road?

boat   ship   scooter

....

7 What word can mean a small animal or a part of a computer?

....

8 (Circle) the odd one out.

keyboard   icon   printer   screen

4 What does this sentence mean? Choose the correct answer: A, B or C.

It might not rain this evening.

A I'm sure it will rain. ☐

B I'm sure it won't rain. ☐

C Perhaps it won't rain. ☐

9 Put the words in order and write the sentence.

buy / to / Mike / new / going / a / computer / isn't

....

....

5 Choose the correct word.

I don't know anything about this film. It *will* / *won't* / *might* be terrible!

10 Choose the correct answer: A, B or C.

Are you going to take the ferry to Corfu?

A Yes, I do.

B Yes, I am.

C Yes, I go.

b 🔊 34 Listen and check your answers.

c Now look at your Student's Book and write three more quiz questions for Unit 5.

Question: ....

....

Answer: ....

Question: ....

....

Answer: ....

Question: ....

....

Answer: ....

6 Xtreme

1 Vocabulary

Extreme sports

a Write the names of the sports. Use a word from each box.

sky	skate
bungee	water
motor	snow
~~mountain~~	scuba

diving (x2)	skiing
racing	boarding (x2)
~~biking~~	jumping

Check it out!

We often use *go + -ing* for sports activities.
Let's go mountain biking next weekend.
She often goes scuba diving in the summer.

1 ..mountain biking..............
2 ....
3 ....
4 ....
5 ....
6 ....
7 ....
8 ....

b Complete the sentences with sports in Exercise 1a.

1 .... is a sport for people who like driving fast.

2 .... and .... are water sports.

3 .... is similar to skateboarding, but it's a winter sport.

4 You fall with your head down when you go ....

5 You need a very strong bicycle for ....

2 Grammar Grammar reference: page 86

should and *shouldn't*

a Match sentences 1–6 with sentences A–F.

1 It's getting late. □
2 Scuba diving is wonderful! □
3 Matt doesn't look good in those jeans. □
4 This cupboard is very heavy. □
5 I think a storm is coming. □
6 My brother is bored at work. □

A You should try it.
B He should look for a different job.
C They shouldn't go out in the boat this morning.
D We should leave soon.
E You shouldn't try to move it on your own.
F He shouldn't wear them.

b Use the table to make five sentences.

You She He We They	should shouldn't	ride eat go out go take	healthier food. to the dentist. it. the bus. this evening.

1 Angela has a problem with her teeth.
 She should go to the dentist.....................

2 We haven't got time to walk to the market.
 ....

3 You look very tired.
 ....

4 Adam has a hamburger and chips for lunch every day.
 ....

5 There's something wrong with their motorbike.
 ....

c Write the questions. Then answer them with *should* or *shouldn't*. Use your own ideas.

1 school / go / he / should / to ?
.Should he go to school?...........................
.No, he shouldn't...........................

2 an / I / should / umbrella / take ?
....
....

3 they / the / should / go / water / in ?
....
....

4 she / what / do / should ?
.What should she do?...........................
.She should go to bed..........................

5 should / road / he / which / choose ?
....
....

6 picnic / I / for / should / what / take / the ?
....
....

Help yourself!

Modals

Should is a **modal** verb. Modals are different from normal verbs because:

• they always go with the infinitive of another verb
• they never change their form
• they never use the auxiliary *do* in questions or negatives.

Which of these are modal verbs?
<u>Underline</u> them.

like   have   will   might   do   can
want   could   go   would   must

(Circle) the correct words.

1 She would *like / likes* an ice cream.
2 Danny *will / wills* come soon.
3 *Do they can / Can they* swim?
4 I *might not / don't might* buy it.
5 What *we should / should we* do?
6 You mustn't *bring / to bring* pets into the hotel.

---

3 **Listen**

a 🔊 **35** Listen and match the speakers (1–4) with the sports. There are two extra sports.

scuba diving ☐   water skiing ☐

skateboarding ☐   snowboarding ☐

bungee jumping ☐   skydiving ☐

b 🔊 **35** Listen again and complete the two sentences for each sport.

1 When you jump, the plane is .... metres from the ground. You can move in all directions while you're ....

2 Don't try this sport before you have .... You must learn to .... under water.

3 The people on TV were jumping off a .... The speaker thinks it looks ....

4 There are special boots so you can't .... your feet on the board. You should also wear .... supports.

4 Vocabulary

Verbs of movement

a Choose two pictures for each verb.

jump	5	
spin		
dive		
climb		
fall		
roll		

b Circle the correct words.

1 They were diving from a rock *into / onto* the water.

2 She fell *off / over* while she was playing basketball.

3 Four skydivers jumped *down / out of* the helicopter.

4 Try to climb *up / over* this rope.

5 I fell *off / out of* my bike this morning.

6 Lisa can spin *up / round* very fast on the ice when she's skating.

7 Let's dive *off / down* the diving board.

8 The horse jumped *up / over* the wall.

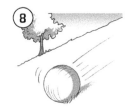

5 Pronunciation

Linking sounds

Check it out!

- When a word ending in *r* comes before a word starting with a vowel, we say the /r/ sound.
  my mother‿and father
- Don't forget, the letter *s* at the end of a word very often has a /z/ sound.

  /z/   /z/   /z/

  These‿are Emma's‿earrings.

a 🔊 36 Draw lines between words with a consonant–vowel link. Listen, check and repeat.

1 Come‿into the house.

2 It's Olga's umbrella.

3 Give Peter a bowl of soup.

4 I woke up at nine o'clock.

5 This is an awful ice cream!

6 It was a hot afternoon in August.

b 🔊 37 Listen to the poem and draw lines to show the linked words.

I climbed up a ladder and fell on the floor.

I jumped off my skateboard and rolled out the door.

I dropped all my books and got wet in the rain ...

Tomorrow I'll do it all over again.

c 🔊 38 Practise saying the whole poem with the recording.

Practise saying these words

🔊 39 climbing   diving board   ground
motor   mountain   practise   roll   shouldn't
skateboarding   skydiving   water skiing   wheel

6 Grammar Grammar reference: page 88

have to and *not have to*

a Match the two parts of the sentences.

1 On European roads
2 When James has exams at university,
3 Our taxi will be here in five minutes, so
4 We've prepared a big meal, so
5 During the holidays
6 Harry can watch the late movie because
7 There's a train station near here, so

A you don't have to bring any food.
B we have to hurry.
C you have to drive on the right.
D they don't have to take the bus.
E he has to study hard.
F students don't have to come to school.
G he doesn't have to get up early tomorrow.

b Complete the sentences with *mustn't* or *don't have to*.

1 You .... dive here.
2 You .... drive faster than 60 kph.
3 You .... turn left.
4 You .... walk up the mountain.
5 You .... take photos here.
6 You .... travel at 30 kph.
7 You .... run in the building.
8 You .... pay any money.

c Complete the sentences. Use the verbs in the box with *mustn't* or the correct form of *have to*.

| wear | touch | ~~look after~~ | forget | work | tidy |

1 I _have to look after_ the baby.

2 She .... today.

3 You .... that!

4 He .... his room.

5 .... I .... this dress?

6 We .... to ring the plumber.

(7) Read

a Read the article quickly and write these words on the picture.

iron   ironing board

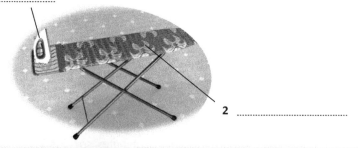

1 ....

2 ....

Extreme ironing

Here's an activity that brings some fun to the world of extreme sports. It's extreme ironing! Danger and adventure come together with housework skills in this strange sport.

The basic equipment is an iron and an ironing board, and the rules are simple. You have to find an unusual outdoor situation, set up your ironing board and iron a few clothes! People do this on the top of mountains and under the sea, in boats and on bicycles. They iron clothes while they are climbing, water skiing, snowboarding, skydiving and even bungee jumping. The board must be at least 1 metre long and you have to use a real iron.

If possible, you should ask somebody to take a photo or make a video of the event.

Englishman Phil Shaw first got the idea for this sport one day when he had a lot of shirts to iron but really wanted to go rock climbing. Extreme ironing now has small groups of supporters in other countries, for example Australia, Japan, Germany and South Africa. Maybe it will be the next Olympic sport! Phil says that extreme ironing gives you all the excitement of an extreme sport together with "the satisfaction of a well-pressed shirt".

Crazy? "Yes, of course it's crazy," says extreme 'ironist' Zoe Phillips. "That's why it's brilliant."

b Are the sentences *right* (✓) or *wrong* (✗)?

1 Extreme ironing is both fun and exciting. ☐

2 You have to use an ironing board for extreme ironing. ☐

3 You can do this sport in your living room if you want to. ☐

4 You don't have to stand on the ground while you are ironing. ☐

5 You have to get a photo or video of the ironing activity. ☐

6 Phil Shaw likes rock climbing. ☐

7 Lots of people from all over the world enjoy extreme ironing. ☐

8 Extreme ironing is going to be part of the next Olympic Games. ☐

Portfolio 6

Describe a sport or game that you like. Write two paragraphs.

Paragraph 1
- Rules – what do you have to do?
- Do you play alone or with other people?

Paragraph 2
- Do you need special clothes or equipment?
- What skills should you have?

Quiz 6

a What do you remember about Unit 6?
Answer all the questions you can and
then check in the Student's Book.

1 Match the words to make four sports.

bungee	skiing
mountain	jumping
water	diving
scuba	biking

....
....
....
....

2 What is the sport in picture A?

....

3 Choose the best answer: A, B or C.

I'd love to try motor racing.

A You shouldn't practise.

B You should wear good running shoes.

C You must know how to drive.

4 There are two mistakes in these
sentences. Write the correct sentences.

Do I should wear a helmet?

Yes, you are.

....
....

5 What is the person doing in picture B?

....

b 🔊 40 Listen and check your answers.

c Now look at your Student's Book and write
three more quiz questions for Unit 6.

6 Are these sentences *right* (✓) or *wrong* (✗)?

When you are zorbing ...

A you roll down a hill.

B you spin in the air.

C you climb up a mountain.

7 Look at the man in picture C. Is he
jumping, diving or falling?

....

8 Circle the correct word.

The picture fell *down* / *off* / *over* the wall.

9 Put the words in order and write the
sentence.

wash / I / dinner / to / have / up / after

....
....

10 Read the answer and complete the question.

When .... ?

I have to leave at 2 o'clock.

Question: ....
....

Answer: ....

Question: ....
....

Answer: ....

Question: ....
....

Answer: ....

7 Sounds good

1 Vocabulary

Music

a Look at the table: 1 is S, 8 is R and 15 is O. Write all these letters in the puzzle. Then complete the music words and write the letters in the table.

1	2	3	4	5	6	7	8	9	10
S							R		

11	12	13	14	15	16	17	18	19
				O				

b Complete the sentences with the words in Exercise 1a.

1 It's a really good song. The music is exciting and the ..lyrics... are great too.

2 This is a single from the band's latest
....

3 I really love the Black Eyed Peas. I'm their biggest
.... !

4 This song was an incredible .... in 2010. In its first week it went straight to number one in the USA, the UK and Australia.

5 Three bands are going to .... at the concert next week.

6 A song by Chris Brown is number one in the .... this week.

7 They didn't .... any songs until 2007, when they got a contract with East West Records.

8 The band will be at the .... every day this week. They're making a new album.

2 Grammar   Grammar reference: page 90

Present perfect and past simple

a Complete the table.

Verb	Past simple	Present perfect
1 take	.took...........	.taken...
2 begin	....	....
3	knew	....
4	....	have bought
5 eat	....	has ....
6	did	....
7	....	spoken
8 write	....	....

b There is a mistake in each of these sentences. Cross out the wrong word(s) and write the correct word(s).

1 We seen Avril Lavigne in concert last year.
....

2 Did you ever played a musical instrument?
....

3 She sings in clubs and concerts, but she didn't record an album.
....

4 Dave has written the lyrics for this song in 2008.
....

5 I never hear this music before.
....

6 Has he bought any CDs at the music shop on Saturday?
....

c 🔊 **41** Complete the conversation with the verbs in the present perfect or the past simple. Then listen and check.

A: ¹ _Have_ you _heard_ (hear) this album? It's fantastic!

B: Oh, it's by Foxy Blues. I ² _____ (see) them a few times on YouTube.

A: I ³ _____ (buy) the CD on Saturday and I love it. I ⁴ _____ (play) it about 50 times!

B: When ⁵ _____ they _____ (record) it?

A: About a month ago. It ⁶ _____ (not get) into the charts, but I'm sure that will happen soon.

B: ⁷ _____ they _____ (make) any other albums?

A: No, they ⁸ _____ . But Ricky Cartland ⁹ _____ (write) some brilliant songs for other bands. Helena Rico ¹⁰ _____ (sing) two of his songs on her album last year.

B: Yes, that's right. I ¹¹ _____ (not like) them much, actually.

A: Oh, really? I ¹² _____ (think) they were great.

Help yourself!

been and gone

Been is the past participle of *be*.
It's **been** cold every day this week.
I've never **been** here before.

Been can also be the past participle of *go*. The verb *go* has two past participles: *been* and *gone*.
She's **gone** to Rome. (= She's still in Rome now.)
She's **been** to Rome. (= She went to Rome in the past but now she's back.)

Complete the sentences with *been* or *gone*.

1 Sorry, Alex is out at the moment. He's _____ to the sports centre.

2 Have you ever _____ to Egypt?

3 I've _____ to Ireland twice. I'd love to go back there.

4 Mum and Dad have _____ to the airport. They're meeting my aunt.

5 Where have you _____? We were looking everywhere for you.

6 Natalie isn't here this weekend. She's _____ skiing with her family.

3 Vocabulary

Music online

a Add vowels (*a, e, i, o, u*) to make words for listening to music online.

1 pdt _____update_____

2 trck _____

3 plylst _____

4 dwnld _____

5 mcrphn _____

6 pld _____

7 cvr rt _____

8 rcrd lbl _____

b Complete the sentences with the words in Exercise 3a.

1 You can _____ this song from the Internet onto your computer.

2 We couldn't hear the singer because her _____ wasn't working.

3 You should _____ your computer operating system. The new system is much faster.

4 Play the first _____ on the album – it's a really nice song.

5 We've made a video and we're going to _____ it onto YouTube.

6 The _____ on the CD includes a great photo of the band in San Francisco.

7 I'm using iTunes to make a _____ of my favourite songs.

8 They've signed a contract with Atlantic Records, which is a really big _____ .

4 Listen

a  42 Listen and match conversations 1–5 with texts A–E.

b 📢 42 Listen again and complete the information in the texts.

A

TRAFFIC HAZARD

THE NEW .... OUT 1ST MAY

Includes the .... Crazy Babe

B

FREE Music Downloads!

Search from over .... songs for your MP3 player.

Our music collection comes to you by agreement with the record ....

Get any song **free** by clicking on DOWNLOAD.

C

File Edit View Insert Format
http://www.goodtunes.co.uk/tigertiger.html

"WHAT ABOUT ME?" ....

★★★★☆

by Tiger Tiger

Album: *The Urban Jungle* (recorded in 20...............)

I stand alone and watch you
The bridge between us burned
What about me, my love? What about me

D

MARIAH CAREY

Friday 18th ....

Only UK concert

Wembley Arena

Tickets on sale 15th ....

E

TICKETLINE

File Edit View Insert Format Tools Actions Help

http://www.ticketline.com/dizzeerascal.html

Event Details

Event:	Dizzee Rascal	⬍
Date/Time:	20 November 19:30	⬍
Venue:	Satellite Arena, ...	⬍

Ticket Details

Top-priced seats	0 ⬍	€148
Best available ticket	0 ⬍	€...............

5 Grammar Grammar reference: page 90

Present perfect with *for* and *since*

a Read Emma's words. Then use the table to make four correct sentences.

> The last time I travelled by plane was in 2008, when I went to Italy. That was my third plane trip to Italy.

She	fly	to Italy	since 2008.
She didn't	flown		in 2008.
She's	flew		last year.
She hasn't			three times.

1 ....
2 ....
3 ....
4 ....

b Complete the sentences with the verbs in the present perfect and (circle) *for* or *since*.

1 You ..*haven't called*.. (not call) me *for* / (*since*) yesterday morning.

2 Marco .... (play) in the band *for* / *since* 2009.

3 We .... (not see) Jess *for* / *since* a few days.

4 They .... (not record) an album *for* / *since* ages.

5 I .... (speak) to Greg three times *for* / *since* we first met.

6 Mrs Fraser .... (teach) at this school *for* / *since* 12 years.

7 .... you .... (be) a member of the club *for* / *since* a long time?

8 Tim .... (not go) to the sports centre *for* / *since* February.

c Write sentences about the pictures in the present perfect.

9:30  NOW: 10:30

1 She / be / on the phone / for

She's been on the phone for an hour.

2004 NOW

2 We / have / our dog / since

7:30  NOW: 3:45

3 She / not eat / since

May  NOW: November

4 I / know / Kristina / for

4:10  NOW: 4:30

5 They / be / in the café / for

1st July 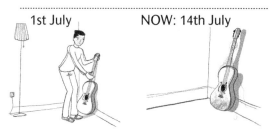 NOW: 14th July

6 He / not practise / the guitar / since

---

6 Pronunciation

/s/ and /z/

a ◀)) **43** Sometimes the letter *c* makes the sound /s/. Tick (✓) the words where *c* is pronounced /s/. Then listen, check and repeat.

| century ☐ | cover ☐ | careful ☐ |

cinema ☐   customer ☐   celebrate ☐

price ☐   difficult ☐   record ☐

medicine ☐   officer ☐   webcam ☐

Look at the words you ticked and complete the rule.

The letter *c* usually makes the sound /s/ when it comes before the vowels .... and ....

b ◀)) **44** Follow the words where the letter *s* is pronounced /z/ to find a way through the puzzle. You can move up and down (↑↓) or left and right (←→). Then listen, check and repeat.

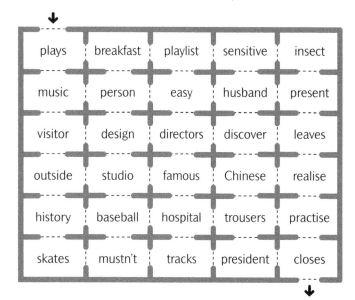

plays	breakfast	playlist	sensitive	insect
music	person	easy	husband	present
visitor	design	directors	discover	leaves
outside	studio	famous	Chinese	realise
history	baseball	hospital	trousers	practise
skates	mustn't	tracks	president	closes

c ◀)) **45** Listen and practise saying the sentences.

1 She's a famous producer.

2 Steve works as a designer.

3 The office isn't open on Tuesdays.

4 Sally is interested in music and science.

5 James has had two hit singles in the charts.

Practise saying these words

◀)) **46** album   company   label   lyrics microphone   opportunity   ordinary   perform producer   professional   sign   voice

⑦ Read

a Read the profile quickly and complete the information in the box.

Alicia Keys

Date of birth: 25th January ¹ ....
First ² .... : Songs in A Minor
First ³ .... : Smokin' Aces

Alicia Keys

Alicia Keys was born in 1981 and grew up in New York. She had music and dance classes when she was a child and she first appeared on TV in *The Cosby Show* at the age of four. She started piano lessons when she was seven and learned classical music before she began to write her own songs at the age of 14.

Alicia signed a contract with J Records in 1999. She recorded several songs for films before her first album, *Songs in A Minor*, came out in 2001. This was a fantastic success. It entered the charts at number one, sold 236,000 copies in its first week, and went on to sell over 12 million copies worldwide. Alicia won five big awards, including Song of the Year for *Fallin'*, the album's top single, which was a number one hit for six weeks.

Since then, Alicia has sold over 30 million albums. She has also become an actress and a record producer with her own studio. She plays the piano as well as singing on all her albums and she has written some great songs for other artists. She has performed in TV programmes and she made her first film, *Smokin' Aces*, in 2007. Her other films include *The Nanny Diaries* (2007) and *The Secret Life of Bees* (2008).

b Choose the correct answer: A, B or C.

1 When she was a child, Alicia Keys
   A lived in New York.
   B often appeared on television.
   C didn't like classical music.

2 She started writing songs
   A for *The Cosby Show*.
   B at the age of seven.
   C in 1995.

3 Her earliest recordings with J Records were
   A before 1999.
   B songs for films.
   C on her first album.

4 *Fallin'* was
   A the name of her first song.
   B a number one album in 2001.
   C at the top of the charts for weeks.

5 Since 2001, Alicia has
   A opened her own studio.
   B started playing the piano.
   C performed all her songs herself.

6 She has had work as a film actress
   A all her life.
   B since 2007.
   C for two years.

Portfolio 7

Write a profile of a musician who interests you. Write two paragraphs.

1 **Early career**
   • Start of music career – how and when?
   • Early success – what and when?

2 **Events since then**
   • How many albums / hit singles?
   • Concerts/tours – where?
   • Other achievements (song writing? films? TV? videos?)

Check it out!

Use the past simple when you are talking about an event which happened <u>at a particular time</u> in the past.

Use the present perfect when you are talking about some time in the period <u>from the past up to now</u>.

He **met** the other members of the band in 2005.
Since then, they **have performed** in concerts all over the world.

Quiz 7

a What do you remember about Unit 7? Answer all the questions you can and then check in the Student's Book.

1 Where is the man in picture A?

....

2 What do we call the words of a song?

....

3 (Circle) the odd one out.

band   single   perform   album

4 What was the name of Rihanna's first album?

....

5 Who is the musician in picture B?

....

6 (Circle) the correct words.

I've chosen two *tracks / charts / playlists* from this website and I'm going to *update / upload / download* them onto my computer.

7 Write the present perfect form of the verbs.

a Kate .... (record) three songs.
b My brothers .... (eat) the chocolate.
c I .... (not begin) my homework.

8 Complete the sentences with the correct form of the verbs.

A: .... you ever .... (see) this band?
B: No, but I .... (hear) them on the radio a few weeks ago.

9 Which two endings are not correct? Cross them out.

She hasn't been here	a since Thursday.
	b for ages.
	c last week.
	d yesterday.
	e before.

10 How do we say the letter *s* in these words? Write /s/ or /z/.

musical ☐   website ☐
instrument ☐   labels ☐

b 🔊 47 Listen and check your answers.

c Now look at your Student's Book and write three more quiz questions for Unit 7.

Question: ....
....
Answer: ....

Question: ....
....
Answer: ....

Question: ....
....
Answer: ....

8 Believe it or not

1 Vocabulary

Adjectives of personality

a Complete the crossword with personality adjectives.

1 An adjective for a person who doesn't tell the truth.
2 Robert is ___ . He likes talking a lot.
3 Some of my friends are like this before exams.
4 Someone who doesn't show good sense is ___ .
5 My sister gives me a lot of presents and helps me with my homework. She's really ___ .
6 Tom is very ___ . He said it was funny when I fell off my bike and hurt my leg.
7 Esteban doesn't like meeting new people and he never talks to anyone at parties. He's ___ .
8 Don't keep these people waiting for more than five minutes.
9 Jon and Paul are very ___ . They watch TV all evening when they should study for their exams.
10 These people have a lot of friends and enjoy meeting people.

b Write the opposites for the words in Exercise 1a.

1 h.................................
2 q.................................
3 e....................... -............................
4 s.................................
5 m.................................
6 s.................................
7 s.................. -...............................
8 p.................................
9 h.................. -...............................
10 u.................................

> **Help yourself!**
>
> **Common adjective endings (2)**
> Here are four more typical endings for adjectives.
>
> -ive   *sensitive*
> -ous   *generous*
> -ent/-ant   *confident, brilliant*
> -able/-ible   *sociable, sensible*
>
> Complete these adjectives with the correct ending and then write them in the lists below.
>
> comfort................   expens................   impati................
> act................   seri................   danger................
> incred................   talkat................   import................
> intellig................   memor................   anxi................
>
> **-ive**   **-ous**
> sensitive   generous
> ....
> ....
> ....
>
> **-ent/-ant**   **-able/-ible**
> confident   sociable
> ....
> ....
> ....
>
> Add other adjectives. Write the lists in your notebook.

2 Grammar Grammar reference: page 92

Zero conditional

a Match the two parts of the sentences.

1 If you want a copy of your document, ☐
2 I get to school late if ☐
3 If you mix blue and yellow, ☐
4 Riding a motorbike is dangerous if ☐
5 Plants die if ☐
6 If I wake up in the middle of the night, ☐
7 If I don't have a big breakfast, ☐

A you get green.
B I often read for half an hour.
C I miss the 8:15 bus.
D I get hungry before lunch time.
E you have to click on PRINT.
F they don't get any water.
G you don't wear a helmet.

b Write sentences. Add *if* and use the zero conditional.

> **Check it out!**
>
> Remember, the *if* clause can come first, or the result clause can come first.

1 I / feel / terrible – I / not get / much sleep
   I feel terrible if I don't get much sleep.
2 I / be / bored at home – I / listen / to music
   ....
   ....
3 people / die – they / not eat
   ....
   ....
4 you / not cook / this dish slowly – it / not taste / nice
   ....
   ....
5 Dad always / get / angry – I / not be / home before 12:00
   ....
   ....
6 Sara / not walk / to work – the weather / be / bad
   ....
   ....

c Complete the sentences. Use your own ideas.

1 If I go to bed late, ...
   ....
2 If people don't eat fruit or vegetables, ...
   ....
3 If you're a sociable person, ...
   ....
4 You can check your emails if ....
   ....
5 If .... ,
   it tastes horrible.

3 Listen

a 🔊 48 Listen. Which adjective is missing in each description? Choose from the adjectives in the box.

| mean | dishonest | generous | shy | hard-working |
| insensitive | lazy | easy-going | impatient | |

1 .... 4 ....
2 .... 5 ....
3 ....

b 🔊 48 Listen again. Are the sentences *right* (✓) *wrong* (✗) or *doesn't say* (–)?

1 Lara is talkative and enjoys meeting people. ☐
2 If there is a problem, Daniel worries about it a lot. ☐
3 Teresa doesn't work hard so she doesn't get good exam results. ☐
4 Greg didn't have any chocolates because his friends ate them all. ☐
5 If you feel unhappy or worried, Nicola is the best person to talk to. ☐

4 Vocabulary

Special days

a Complete the sentences with the names of the festivals.

Thanksgiving   the Day of the Dead   Eid   Diwali
Hanukkah   Christmas   New Year's Eve

1 On the last day of .... we have a big meal and we light nine candles in a special candlestick.

2 At midnight on .... we celebrate with singing, dancing and fireworks.

3 .... is the festival of light, so everyone lights candles, lamps and fireworks.

4 At .... we have lots to eat and drink. Before this time, we don't eat anything during the day for a whole month.

5 At .... time we put decorations in our houses and we have a decorated tree.

6 .... is an autumn festival when families have a traditional meal together.

7 On .... we remember people in our families who have died. We believe they come back to visit us on this day.

b Are the sentences *right* (✓) or *wrong* (✗)?

1 People give each other presents at Christmas. ☐

2 The biggest celebrations for the Day of the Dead are in Mexico. ☐

3 People usually eat chicken at Thanksgiving. ☐

4 There are always fireworks at Hanukkah. ☐

5 People celebrate Diwali in India. ☐

6 Eid is a traditional South American festival. ☐

7 New Year's Eve is on the first day of January. ☐

5 Grammar Grammar reference: page 92

First conditional

a Choose the correct answer: A, B, C or D.

- If ¹........... further up the hill, ²........... able to see the fireworks.
- If you ³........... to the festival next month, ⁴........... a great time.
- Carla ⁵........... disappointed if her team ⁶........... tomorrow.
- Where ⁷........... if ⁸........... to Barcelona?
- If Paolo ⁹........... later, ¹⁰........... the phone?

1 A we walk	**B** we'll walk	**C** will we walk	**D** we won't walk
2 A we were	**B** we'll be	**C** we won't	**D** we aren't
3 A come	**B** came	**C** comes	**D** will come
4 A you have	**B** you're having	**C** you had	**D** you'll have
5 A is	**B** isn't	**C** will be	**D** will have
6 A wins	**B** doesn't win	**C** will win	**D** won't win
7 A Anna stays	**B** Anna will stay	**C** will Anna stay	**D** Anna will she stay
8 A she'll go	**B** does she go	**C** will she go	**D** she goes
9 A ring	**B** rings	**C** will ring	**D** will he ring
10 A you answer	**B** do you answer	**C** will answer you	**D** will you answer

b Complete the sentences. Use the correct form of the verbs.

> they / not run   ~~I / finish / this painting today~~   you / find / some lemonade
> the rain / stop   he / not be / careful   we / be / late

1 .I'll finish this painting today. if I work hard.

2 She'll play tennis this afternoon if ....

3 If the train doesn't come soon, ...

4 If you look in the fridge, ...
....

5 He'll fall off his bike if ....
....

6 If... ,
they won't catch the bus.

c 🔊 **49** Complete the conversations with the correct form of the verbs. Then listen and check.

> Maria: It's Patrick's party tomorrow. Are you going?
> Nadia: Maybe – I'm not sure. I¹ ..'ll go. (go) if Pietro ² .... (come) with me. If he ³ .... (have to) work, I'll probably stay at home.
> Maria: What ⁴............... you .... (wear) if you decide to go?
> Nadia: My red dress, probably.

> Tim: ⁵................ you .... (watch) the motor racing if it ⁶............................. (be) on TV next weekend?
> Dave: I'd like to, but if we ⁷............................. (have) football practice, I ⁸............................. (not be) home in time. Anyway, that's OK. If I ⁹............................. (not be) here, my sister ¹⁰............................. (record) it for me.

> Luke: It's getting late. Where's Julie?
> Petra: I don't know. I tried to phone her. If she ¹¹............................. (not come) soon, I ¹²............................. (phone) her again.
> Luke: What ¹³............... we .... (do) if she ¹⁴............................. (not get) here?
> Petra: We'll just have to leave without her.

6 Pronunciation

Syllables

a 🔊 **50** Listen and write the number of syllables: 1, 2, 3 or 4.

mis<u>take</u>	..2..	patient	....
festival	....	serious	....
fire	....	superstition	....
intelligent	....	upset	....
midnight	....	watched	....
important	....	insensitive	....
celebration	....	unlucky	....

b 🔊 **50** Listen again. In the words of more than one syllable, <u>underline</u> the main stress. Listen, check and repeat.

c 🔊 **51** Listen and practise saying the sentences.

1 Nick is nice.
2 <u>Pat</u>rick is <u>pat</u>ient.
3 Ra<u>quel</u> is re<u>laxed</u>.
4 <u>Jen</u>nifer is <u>gen</u>erous.
5 Ro<u>ber</u>to is ro<u>man</u>tic.
6 An<u>gel</u>ica is in<u>tel</u>ligent.

> **Practise saying these words**
>
> 🔊 **52** anxious   Christmas   decision
> dishonest   energy   excellent   impatient
> laugh   monkey   natural   skeleton

⑦ Read

a Read the paragraph at the top of the quiz. Then tick (✓) the correct sentence.

A Modern technology makes it easy to predict the weather.

B Weather predictions were better in the past than now.

C We don't predict the weather very successfully now.

b Now do the quiz. Choose one answer: A, B or C.

Weather superstitions

Today, 'super computers' for predicting the weather can make almost 70 trillion calculations per second – but we still can't be sure what the weather will do in a few days' time. In the past, it was even more difficult, and every country has its ancient superstitions to try to predict the weather.

This quiz is about some of the old weather sayings in the UK and the USA. Can you guess the answers?

1 If you see cows lying down in a field,

A the day will be windy.

B there will be fog at night.

C it will rain soon.

2 If a cat sits with its back to the fire, it will be

A cloudy.

B cold.

C hot.

3 Frogs make more noise than usual

A before a storm.

B when it's raining.

C when the sun goes behind clouds.

4 If you see dolphins swimming north,

A you'll get good weather.

B there will be rain in the south.

C there will be a storm at sea.

5 If birds fly low,

A warm weather will soon arrive.

B the weather will be rainy.

C it won't rain for three days.

6 If the wind comes from the south on New Year's Day, there will be

A snow in January.

B a hard year to come.

C good weather in the year to come.

7 If this year's onions have thin skins, the winter

A will be freezing.

B won't be very cold.

C won't have much rain.

8 Potatoes and carrots won't grow well if you plant them

A when the moon shines at night.

B when the weather is very warm.

C after a storm.

c 🔊 **53** Listen and check your answers. The average score for this quiz is 4 correct answers out of 8. How well did you do?

d Do you have any of these superstitions in your country? Do you believe any of them? Prepare to talk about this in your next class. Make notes to help you.

Portfolio 8

Translate six superstitions from your country. Choose six of these topics:

- good weather
- bad weather
- good luck
- bad luck
- money
- getting married
- dying
- New Year

Quiz 8

a What do you remember about Unit 8? Answer all the questions you can and then check in the Student's Book.

1 Add vowels (*a, e i, o, u*) to make personality adjectives.

gnrs ....

scbl ....

dshnst ....

6 Where do most people celebrate Diwali?

....

2 Circle the odd one out.

relaxed   anxious   easy-going
self-confident

7 Circle the correct verbs.

If *you live / you'll live* in Australia, Christmas *came / comes* in the summer.

3 Write the opposites of these adjectives.

lucky   ....

patient   ....

sensitive   ....

8 Complete the sentence.

If I .... (not see) Fiona this afternoon, I .... (phone) her tonight.

9 There are two mistakes in this sentence. Write the correct sentence.

We have a picnic on the beach tomorrow if the weather will be nice.

....

....

....

4 What three animals can you see in picture A?

....

....

5 What is the festival in picture B?

....

10 How many syllables are there in these words?

talkative ☐   relaxed ☐   celebration ☐

b 🔊 54 Listen and check your answers.

c Now look at your Student's Book and write three more quiz questions for Unit 8.

Question: ....

....

Answer: ....

Question: ....

....

Answer: ....

Question: ....

....

Answer: ....

9 What does she look like?

1 Vocabulary

Describing appearance

a Put the letters in the correct order and write the adjectives in the puzzle. Put the ○ letters in order to make one more adjective to describe appearance.

b Write the words from Exercise 1a in the correct list.

General appearance	Size
.good-looking...........	.little...........

Shape	Hair
.square...........	.short...........

1 TAF

2 TSOHR

3 LDBA

4 GYUL

5 TEUC

6 NETDIOP

7 DONRU

8 TIHGSTRA

9 VYAW

> **Check it out!**
>
> He's bald. He's got a bald head.
> **not** ~~He's got bald hair.~~

c Circle the correct words.

Robbie [1]*is / has got* dark, [2]*wavy / curly* hair and [3]*big / long* eyes. He's very [4]*ugly / cute*.

Zoë's got [5]*long / short* hair and a long, [6]*round / pointed* nose. I don't think she's very [7]*beautiful / bald*, but all her friends think she looks great.

Mr Freeman has got [8]*pretty / little*, round eyes and [9]*he's / he's got* bald. He isn't [10]*good-looking / overweight*, but he's fun and very interesting.

2 Grammar Grammar reference: page 94

Question tags

a Choose the correct answer: A, B or C.

1 He's an engineer, ...
   A is it?   **B** isn't it?   **C** isn't he?

2 They can hear us, ...
   A can't they?   **B** don't they?   **C** don't we?

3 She's got blonde hair, ...
   A isn't she?   **B** hasn't she?   **C** doesn't she?

4 I'm a bit overweight, ...
   A am I?   **B** don't I?   **C** aren't I?

5 You haven't been to Australia, ...
   A were you?   **B** have you?   **C** are you?

6 You don't know my cousin, ...
   A do you?   **B** aren't you?   **C** don't you?

7 It will probably rain later, ...
   A will it?   **B** won't it?   **C** isn't it?

8 He enjoys skiing, ...
   A doesn't he?   **B** isn't he?   **C** hasn't he?

b 🔊 **55** Complete the conversations with question tags. Then listen and check.

A: Hey, those are new shoes, ¹ *aren't they* ?
B: Yeah, I bought them yesterday. They look good, ² _____ ?

A: This soup doesn't taste very good, ³ _____ ?
B: Ugh! It's got too much salt in it, ⁴ _____ ?

A: We should leave soon, ⁵ _____ ?
B: Oh, there's no hurry. It's only 6:30, ⁶ _____ ?

A: You haven't brought those books, ⁷ _____ ?
B: Oh, no – sorry. I'll bring them tomorrow.

③ Vocabulary

On TV

a Match the types of programme with the pictures.

| drama series | the news | quiz show |
| documentary | chat show | comedy series |

1 _____

2 _____

3 _____

4 _____

5 _____

6 _____

b Ⓒircle the correct words.

1 A comedy series is *funny / serious*.
2 A quiz show is a *competition / sports event* on TV.
3 A soap opera is a continuing story that often follows the lives of *famous / ordinary* people.
4 On a chat show famous people *give interviews / talk to journalists* in the studio.
5 We watch the news to find out about *the past / recent events*.
6 Documentaries give us information about *TV characters / things in the real world*.
7 A drama series usually has *an exciting story / a funny ending*.
8 People make an advertisement because they want to make us *laugh / buy something*.

4 Pronunciation

Question tags

a 🔊 **56** Listen and tick (✓) the correct meaning.

	Not sure ⤴	Sure ⤵
1 The news is on soon, **isn't it?**	☐	☐
2 Tom doesn't like quiz shows, **does he?**	☐	☐
3 They'll show the football on Channel 2, **won't they?**	☐	☐
4 You haven't seen this show, **have you?**	☐	☐
5 Jill can play the piano, **can't she?**	☐	☐
6 We don't have to leave now, **do we?**	☐	☐

> **Practise saying these words**
>
> 🔊 **58** advertisement   bald   character
> comedy   cute   documentary   immediately
> jewellery   manager   overweight   pretty   round

b 🔊 **57** Do you think the intonation will go up (⤴) or down (⤵) in the question tags? Listen, check and repeat.

1 I don't know much about this programme. It's a documentary, **isn't it**?

2 Alice is a big fan of the Jonas Brothers. She'll love this CD, **won't she**?

3 Who's that character? We haven't seen him before, **have we**?

4 Let's watch something else. This isn't very good, **is it**?

5 I can't remember where Liam's house is. He lives near the river, **doesn't he**?

5 Read

a Read the text from a TV guide and answer the questions.

TVA1	TVA2	RTV
6:00 News at Six National and international news presented by Olivia Sanders. Including sport and weather.	**6:00 The Name Game** Ben Logan presents the popular general knowledge quiz.	**6:10 Friends and Family** Will Damian ask for help before it is too late? Zac wants Melissa to come home. Katie is upset with Frank.
	6:30 Wally's World Lots of laughs when Wally tries to keep a dog in his apartment.	**6:40 RTV News Update** From the RTV news team.
7:00 Island of Dreams Presenter Stephen Bold makes a journey to Indonesia to look at the art and culture of beautiful Bali.	**7:00 LA Cops** Part 3 in the documentary series that follows the daily lives of officers in the Los Angeles police force.	**7:00 Plat du Jour** French chef Jules Vernet looks at the classic dishes of Provence and shows us how to make a fabulous fish soup.
8:00 The Grace Lawson Show Grace's guests in the studio include actor Will Smith and pop star Lady Gaga.	**8:00 Rossiter** A professional killer is somewhere in London and Inspector Rossiter has only 24 hours to find him.	**8:00 Worldwatch: *Going Nowhere*** A report by Anna Murray looks at public transport in Europe and discovers some surprising facts.

1 What kind of programme starts on RTV at 6:10?   ....

2 How many documentaries are on between 6:00 and 9:00?   ....

3 Which channels are showing the news?   ....

4 Which programme is part of a comedy series?   ....

5 What kind of programme is on after the documentary on TVA2?   ....

6 When can you watch a cooking show?   ....

7 What kind of programme is showing at 8:00 on TVA1?   ....

8 Is Anna Murray an actress, a character or a journalist?   ....

b Which programmes in the TV guide would you like to watch? Why? Prepare to talk about this in your next class. Make notes to help you.

6 Grammar Grammar reference: page 96

Defining relative clauses

a Circle the correct word.

1 I've got two friends *who / which* come from Poland.

2 Stratford is the town *which / where* Shakespeare was born.

3 We stayed in a hotel *who / which* was very near the beach.

4 I read the email *who / that* you sent to Daniel.

5 She's someone *that / where* my parents met in Switzerland.

6 I want a camera *which / where* is very easy to use.

7 We haven't met the people *who / which* are living in flat 4.

8 This is the street *that / where* they have the market on Saturdays.

Check it out!

In a relative clause with *where*, there must always be a subject between *where* and the verb.

*I like the street **where** <u>we</u> live.*

*That's the café **where** <u>Sophie</u> works.*

b Complete the sentences with *who*, *which*, *that* or *where*. Sometimes two answers are possible.

1 We're going to watch the quiz show .... starts at 7:30.

2 Mustafa is a TV journalist .... works for Channel 2.

3 I'm looking for a shop .... I can buy some good olive oil.

4 My brother knows some of the actors .... are in this soap opera.

5 This is the watch .... Lucy gave me for my birthday.

6 We visited the village in France .... Dad used to live.

c Write sentences for the pictures. Use words from each column.

He's a footballer		fly south for the winter.
That's the shop		Grandma wore in the 1960s.
It's a documentary about birds	who	John's band used to play.
	which	plays for Juventus in Italy.
We found a dress	that	They've closed the club	where	won first prize in the competition.
Teresa is the girl		I bought my bike.

1 <u>We found a dress which Grandma wore in the 1960s.</u>

2 ....

3 ....

4 ....

5 ....

6 ....

⑦ Listen

a 🔊 **59** Listen to the radio quiz. Which person has the most correct answers?

Michael ☐   Karen ☐   James ☐

b 🔊 **59** Listen again. Are the sentences *right* (✓) or *wrong* (✗)?

Quiz question 1

1 Hannah Montana is an actress who first appeared in a TV series. ☐

2 The series which the actress starred in was on television in 2005. ☐

3 Miley Cyrus wasn't a famous film star before 2006. ☐

Quiz question 2

4 The TV comedy series began in 1998. ☐

5 The quiz question is about a character who isn't good-looking. ☐

Quiz question 3

6 About half a billion people watch the World Cup every year. ☐

7 The football World Cup is an event that takes place in Brazil. ☐

8 South Africa is the country where they had the 2010 World Cup. ☐

Portfolio 9

**Choose two of the photos and describe the people.
Include the following information.**

- general appearance (*pretty / good-looking …*)
- age (*about 25 / middle-aged …*)
- hair (*short / straight …*)
- other details (*a long nose / pointed ears …*)
- your ideas about their personality (*He/She looks intelligent / self-confident …*)

Quiz 9

a What do you remember about Unit 9? Answer all the questions you can and then check in the Student's Book.

1 Complete the sentence.

The man in picture A is b_____ .

2 Circle the odd one out.

ugly   pretty   beautiful   good-looking

3 Circle the correct words.

a A more polite word for *fat* is *round* / *overweight*.

b The word *pointed* can describe a dog's nose or *eyes* / *ears* / *hair*.

4 The woman in picture B is a look-alike. Who is the real person?

_____

5 Match the statements with the question tags.

1 You'll record this show for me,   **A** haven't you?

2 You've seen the film before,   **B** don't you?

3 You love soap operas,   **C** won't you?

6 Complete the sentences with question tags.

A: Steve looks like his father, _____ ?

B: Yes, but they haven't got the same eyes, _____ ?

7 Should the intonation go up or down in this question tag?

My name isn't on the list, so I'm not in the team, am I?

8 What is the type of programme in picture C? Choose two words.

show   comedy   quiz   series
chat   news   drama

_____   _____

9 Choose the correct answer: A, B or C.

A soap opera

A is a type of advertisement.

B sometimes continues for years.

C gives us facts and information.

10 There is a mistake in each of these sentences. ~~Cross out~~ the wrong word and write the correct word.

Franz is a student which comes from Germany.   _____

I met him at the sports club that I play tennis.   _____

b 🔊 60 Listen and check your answers.

c Now look at your Student's Book and write three more quiz questions for Unit 9.

Question: _____
_____
Answer: _____

Question: _____
_____
Answer: _____

Question: _____
_____
Answer: _____

10 Getting around

1 Grammar Grammar reference: page 96

Verb + -ing and verb + infinitive

a Complete the sentences with the correct form of the verb.

1 Do you want ..to come....... (come) to the airport with us?

2 I don't enjoy .... (play) football.

3 They finished .... (record) their first album in July.

4 You'll need .... (buy) a ticket before you get on the bus.

5 Mike decided .... (take) the ferry to Ireland.

6 I don't mind .... (cook), but I hate .... (wash) the dishes.

b Some sentences are correct, but some have mistakes. Tick (✓) the correct sentences. ~~Cross out~~ the mistakes and write the correct words.

1 Eva started playing the guitar when she was eight. ..✓....................

2 They agreed ~~meeting~~ at 7:30 outside the cinema. ..to meet.................

3 We like travelling by train. ....

4 Andrew learned to ski when he was on holiday in France. ....

5 I don't mind to listen to classical music. ....

6 They began to make plans for their trip to Turkey. ....

7 Ben doesn't enjoy to watch soap operas on TV. ....

8 My sister hopes becoming an architect after her university course. ....

c Write true sentences about these topics.

1 something you enjoy doing
....

2 something you need to do soon
....

3 something you will continue to do next year
....

4 something you haven't finished doing
....

5 something you hope to do in the future
....

2 Vocabulary

Travel verbs

a Complete the sentences with travel verbs.

1 They're ..getting off. the plane.

2 He's .... his car.

3 The plane is ....

4 He's .... the train.

5 She's .... a car.

6 They're going to .... the bus.

7 She's .... a motorbike.

8 The plane is ....

b There is a mistake in each of these sentences. ~~Cross out~~ the wrong word and write the correct word.

1 I got on the train at Cambridge and took off at King's Cross station. ....

2 It was very foggy at the airport, but the plane grounded safely. ....

3 He got on his motorbike and drove it to the shopping centre. ....

4 It was raining heavily when they got out off the taxi. ....

5 We got on the plane at about 6:00, but it didn't take up until 6:30. ....

6 There's a bus stop at the station where you can reach the bus to the city centre.

....

3 Grammar Grammar reference: page 96

Infinitive of purpose and *for* + noun

a Match the two parts of the sentences.

1 I go running every morning ☐

2 Mum is ringing the restaurant ☐

3 I looked on the internet ☐

4 Danny has gone to the supermarket ☐

5 You don't need special sports equipment ☐

6 Dad is coming to the bus station ☐

7 We had a big party ☐

A to find the cheapest flights to Lisbon.

B to do the week's shopping.

C to pick me up.

D to keep fit.

E to celebrate my uncle's 40th birthday.

F to make a reservation for dinner.

G to play volleyball.

b Complete the sentences. Use the words in the box with *for*.

| some milk | the printer | his website | the picnic | my History project | his trip to the USA |

1 My cousin has got his ticket ....

2 We need some more paper ....

3 I'm getting some information ....

4 Adam has designed a new page ....

5 Sandro has gone to the shop ....

6 We've made some sandwiches ....

C  **61** Complete the conversation with *to* or *for*. Then listen and check.

Kelly: We should get together ¹............ make some plans ²............ our skiing trip. Do you want to come over?

Alice: No, not right now. I'm going into town ³............ buy a few things. I need some new boots ⁴............ the winter, and I might go into Sadler's ⁵............ have a look at their jumpers. Why don't you come with me?

Kelly: No, thanks – I hate shopping ⁶............ clothes. I'll meet you later at the café ⁷............ an ice cream if you like.

Alice: Right. I'll see you there at four o'clock, OK?

4 Read

Read the article and choose the correct answer: A, B or C.

The world's first travel agent

In the 1840s there were no cars or planes, and trains were a strange new invention. Only a few rich people could travel to other countries for holidays. Most people stayed close to the place where they lived. But in 1841 an Englishman, Thomas Cook, had an idea that changed things completely.

Thomas was walking from his home to a nearby town when he first thought of using the new railways to run a group tour. He organised a return train trip for 570 passengers to travel from Leicester to Loughborough, a distance of 20 km. The day was a great success, and in the following years Thomas continued to organise 'Cook's tours' at quite low prices to places in the UK.

His tours reached Europe in 1855 and the USA in 1868. A year later he began taking people to Egypt to sail up the Nile. Then in 1872 he organised the first round-the-world tour. Thomas and his group of tourists were away for 222 days and travelled more than 40,000 km.

All these international tours included transport (by ship, train and coach) and arrangements for hotel rooms and meals. This was amazing at a time when there were no phones or computers for quick communication. Thomas also wrote books of travel information for his customers.

When Thomas Cook died in 1892, the world was open to many thousands of new travellers. Today we spend about 645 billion euros a year on tourism. It is the world's biggest business.

1 In the 1840s
  A there weren't any trains.
  B only rich people could take holiday flights.
  C it was expensive to travel to other countries.

2 At that time most people
  A didn't have any holidays.
  B didn't travel far from home.
  C didn't like travelling.

3 Thomas Cook started thinking about organising a group tour
  A in 1841.
  B while he was walking home.
  C while he was on a train.

4 On the first trip that Thomas organised, people
  A travelled more than 500 kilometres.
  B got on a train at Leicester.
  C spent the night at Loughborough.

5 Between 1841 and 1855, his customers
  A travelled in the UK.
  B made trips to Europe.
  C paid a lot of money for their tours.

6 On the tour in 1872, his group of tourists
  A were the first people to go around the world.
  B took nearly eight months to finish the journey.
  C had to find hotels to stay in.

7 Thomas Cook
  A had a slow computer.
  B wrote books about the people who went on his tours.
  C died before the end of the century.

(5) Vocabulary

Going on a trip

(a) Complete the crossword. Use the picture clues to help you.

Across

 ②

 ③

window ....

⑤
TICKETS

⑦

ticket ....

Down

①

②

④

⑥

..............-.............. desk

(b) Complete the sentences with the words in Exercise 5a.

1 We need to look at a .... to find out when the buses leave.

2 I bought my ticket to Edinburgh at the .... in the bus station.

3 The New York train is arriving at .... 3.

4 I always sit in a .... if I can. I like looking out at the countryside.

5 On this flight, if your .... weighs more than 15 kg, you have to pay extra money.

6 Always carry your .... in a safe place when you're travelling.

7 When you're taking a flight, go to the .... desk first.

8 All passengers have to go through a .... check before they can get on the plane. This is to make sure the flight is safe.

(6) Pronunciation

Diphthongs: /eɪ/, /əʊ/ and /aɪ/

(a) 🔊 62 Listen and tick (✓) the word you hear.

short vowel		/eɪ/	
1 plan	☐	plane	☐
2 hat	☐	hate	☐
3 snack	☐	snake	☐

short vowel		/əʊ/	
4 hop	☐	hope	☐
5 got	☐	goat	☐
6 Rod	☐	road	☐

short vowel		/aɪ/	
7 Tim	☐	time	☐
8 did	☐	died	☐
9 chin	☐	China	☐

b 🔊 **63** Find two ways through the puzzle. Follow the words which contain /eɪ/ sounds and /aɪ/ sounds. Then listen, check and repeat.

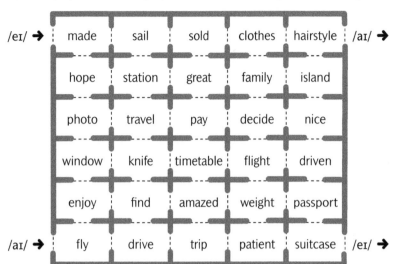

/eɪ/ →	made	sail	sold	clothes	hairstyle	/aɪ/ →
	hope	station	great	family	island	
	photo	travel	pay	decide	nice	
	window	knife	timetable	flight	driven	
	enjoy	find	amazed	weight	passport	
/aɪ/ →	fly	drive	trip	patient	suitcase	/eɪ/ →

c 🔊 **64** Listen and practise saying the sentences.

1 Jane's paintings are amazing.
2 They hate making mistakes.
3 Tony has broken the window.
4 Don't go out in those old clothes.
5 I might fly to China.
6 Simon likes riding his bike at night.

Practise saying these words

🔊 **65** climate   continue
explorer   journey   knock
office   passenger   protect
security   suitcase
temperature   through

7 Listen

🔊 **66** Listen to the five recordings. Choose the correct answer: A, B or C.

1 Where was she at half past two?

A ☐   B ☐   C ☐

4 How does he feel about the bus trip?

A ☐   B ☐   C ☐

2 Which is the place for the Liverpool train?

PLATFORM 6   PLATFORM 2   PLATFORM 4

A ☐   B ☐   C ☐

5 Which timetable are they looking at?

A ☐   B ☐   C ☐

3 What did he lose?

A ☐   B ☐   C ☐

Portfolio 10

Imagine you are a tourist visiting your area for the first time. You arrived this morning and now it is evening. Write an email to a friend. Write two paragraphs.

1 This morning
- How did you travel?
- Where is your hotel and how did you get there?

2 This afternoon
- Where did you go and how did you get there?
- What did you see?
- Did you enjoy it?

Quiz 10

a What do you remember about Unit 10? Answer all the questions you can and then check in the Student's Book.

1 What world record does Rob Thomson hold?

....

2 How long did the woman in picture A take to run around the world?

....

3 Complete the sentences with the correct form of the verbs.

I really want .... (learn) .... (play) the piano. I don't mind .... (practise) every day.

4 One sentence is incorrect. ~~Cross it out.~~

A She started put her clothes in the suitcase.

B She started to put her clothes in the suitcase.

C She started putting her clothes in the suitcase.

5 Look at picture B and ⟨circle⟩ the correct words.

He's getting *into / off / out of* the car and she's getting *in / on / out of* the bus.

6 Use these letters to make three travel verbs. Write them with the nouns.

c d h r v i t e a c

.... a car .... a scooter

.... a train

7 Complete the sentence.

I'm going to the shops .... buy a present .... my aunt's birthday.

8 Which word has a different vowel sound?

take sail hate crash railway

9 Use letters from each box to make words for going on a trip.

sec	tim	sui	pas		tca	sp	ur	eta

ort	ity	ble	se

....

....

10 Tick (✓) the things you can see at a station.

ticket office ☐ check-in desk ☐

timetable ☐ platform ☐

b 🔊 67 Listen and check your answers.

c Now look at your Student's Book and write three more quiz questions for Unit 10.

Question: ....

....

Answer: ....

Question: ....

....

Answer: ....

Question: ....

....

Answer: ....

11 Lights, camera, action!

1 Vocabulary

Films

a Add vowels (*a, e, i, o, u*) to make film words. Write them in the correct list.

> drctr   scrpt   stnt prsn   flm str   cmr prtr
> xtr   lctn   mk-p rtst   st

People

....

....

....

Things and places

....

....

....

b Complete the sentences with the words in Exercise 1a.

The ¹.. is reading her
².. while the
³.. is working.

The film-makers are on ⁴..
in England. A ⁵.. is falling
off a horse and a ⁶.. is
filming the action.

The main actors aren't here yet. There are lots of
⁷.. in this scene and the
⁸.. is talking to them.
The street looks real, but it's actually a
⁹.. in the studio.

2 Grammar Grammar reference: page 98

Present simple passive

a Complete the sentences with the verbs in the present passive.

1 Lots of popular musicals ..*are made*.. (make) in India.

2 In this recipe, the meat .... (cook) slowly for two hours.

3 Special effects .... (create) by computers.

4 Foreign films .... often .... (show) at this cinema.

5 English and French .... (speak) in Canada.

6 That type of knife .... (not use) for cutting bread.

7 Cheese .... often .... (not eat) in China.

8 These facts .... (not know) by many people.

b Write the questions and complete the answers.

1 **A:** lemon tea / drink / with milk?

..*Is lemon tea drunk with milk?*.............

B: No, ..*it isn't*.............................

2 **A:** football / play / in South America?

....

B: Yes, ...

3 **A:** these machines / make / in Germany?

....

....

B: Yes, ...

4 **A:** this dessert / serve / with ice cream?

....

B: No, ...

5 **A:** newspapers / sell / at the supermarket?

....

....

B: No, ...

6 **A:** crocodiles / find / in Australia?

....

....

B: Yes, ...

c Read the answers. Then use the table to make the questions.

Where is	the late movie	called?
How are	tigers	found?
What are	Portuguese	made?
When is	the magazines	spoken?
Where are	chips	shown?

1 ....

They're called *Elle* and *Vogue*.

2 ....

In Portugal and Brazil.

3 ....

By cooking potatoes in oil.

4 ....

In parts of Asia.

5 ....

Every night at 11:30.

3 Listen

a 🔊 68 Listen to the radio quiz. Match the questions with the correct topics.

Question 1 ☐
Question 2 ☐
Question 3 ☐

A art
B food or drink
C fashion
D famous people
E sport
F films
G television

b 🔊 68 Listen again and answer the three quiz questions.

1 ....

2 ....

3 ....

c 🔊 69 Now listen to the full recording and check your answers.

d Write your own question for the quiz. Describe a thing, a place or an activity. Bring your quiz question to your next class.

....

....

....

4 Vocabulary

Materials

a Make eight words for materials. Use one letter from each column.

¹G	L	A	S	S		²				
³					⁴					
⁵					⁶					
⁷					⁸					

```
    M  L  A  S̶            O  O  T  D
    P̶  D  S̶  S  A         R  E  B  O  H
    A  R  K̶  B  O  T  I  D   W  U  A  B  N  E
    C  Ø  P  E  T  A  L  R  C  C  L  T  O  T  E  R  R
```

b Write the materials for the things in the pictures.

1 ....

2 ....

3 ....

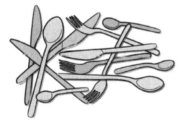

4 ....

5 ....

6 ....

7 ....

8 ....

> **Check it out!**
>
> Most of the words for materials can be used as adjectives as well as nouns.
>
> *The bottle is made of **glass**.* (noun)
> *It's a **glass** bottle.* (adjective)
>
> However, the adjective for *wood* is *wooden*.
> *The chairs are made of **wood**.*
> *They're **wooden** chairs.*

5 Grammar

Grammar reference: page 98

Past simple passive

a There is a mistake in each of these sentences. ~~Cross out~~ the wrong word(s) and write the correct word(s).

1 The first phone call is made in 1876.

....

2 The building was finish six months ago.

....

3 These photos took in New York in 2008.

....

4 Jeans aren't wore in the 18th century.

....

5 Were the letters send to the wrong address?

....

6 The race didn't win by an American.

....

7 When you are born?

....

8 The film was seen from millions of people around the world.

....

> **Check it out!**
>
> When we are referring to the past, we always use *was* or *were* with *born*.
>
> *I was born in Barcelona.*
> **not** ~~I'm born~~ or ~~I born~~

b Complete the text. Use the verbs in the past passive form.

The Dark Knight, one of my favourite films,
¹_____ (show) for the first time
in 2008. The film ²_____ (direct)
by Christopher Nolan, who also helped to write
the script. It ³_____ (base) on a
story which ⁴_____ (write) by
Christopher's brother, Jonathan.
   The main characters, Batman and The Joker,
⁵_____ (play) by Christian Bale and
Heath Ledger. I thought the acting was great and the
camera work was excellent. The scenes in Gotham
City ⁶_____ (film) brilliantly and
wonderful special effects ⁷_____
(create) by stunt people and CGI.

c Rewrite the sentences in the passive. The underlined words should be the subject of the sentence.

1 They didn't use stunt people in this film.
 .Stunt people weren't used in this film...................

2 When did they open the new sports centre?
 .When was the new sports centre opened?...............

3 Someone recorded that song five years ago.
 .That song...

4 They sold the paintings for £20,000.
 ....

5 People didn't make this film in Hollywood.
 ....
 ....

6 They didn't begin work on the series until March 2009.
 ....
 ....

7 Did someone invent mobile phones in the 1960s?
 ....
 ....

8 Where did they film the documentary?
 ....
 ....

6 Pronunciation

-ed in regular past participles: /t/, /d/ and /ɪd/

a 🔊70 Write the number of syllables: 1, 2 or 3. Then listen, check and repeat.

filmed ☐   reached ☐   needed ☐
picked ☐   hated ☐   invented ☐
returned ☐   repeated ☐
included ☐   followed ☐

b 🔊71 Listen and tick (✓) the sound of the *-ed* ending. Then listen again and repeat.

	/t/	/d/	/ɪd/
1 trained as a stunt person	☐	☐	☐
2 recorded in the studio	☐	☐	☐
3 cooked in the kitchen	☐	☐	☐
4 reported on the news	☐	☐	☐
5 watched in the cinema	☐	☐	☐
6 painted on the wall	☐	☐	☐

Check it out!

The *-ed* ending is usually pronounced /d/.
showed   trained   filmed   sailed
covered   carried (etc.)

It is pronounced /t/ when it follows these sounds:
/f/   *laughed*   /s/   *placed, missed, mixed*
/k/   *looked*   /ʃ/   *crashed, watched*
/p/   *stopped*

It is pronounced /ɪd/ when it follows these sounds:
/d/   *added*   /t/   *invented*

c 🔊72 Listen and practise saying the sentences.

1 The work was started but it wasn't finished.
2 The house is watched and protected by the police.
3 The songs were performed and recorded.

Practise saying these words

🔊73 cardboard   cotton   director   expert
explosion   false   leather   location
operator   safety   scissors

(7) Read

a Read Robbie's blog and match the film titles with the photos.

1 ☐ *What Happens in Vegas*

2 ☐ *Terminator Salvation*

3 ☐ *Street Fighter*

A

B

C

FILM REVIEWS

http://www.RobbiesBlogspot.net/filmreviews

Robbie's Blogspot

11:30 Tuesday June 16

What are the worst films you've seen? Here's a list of some of mine.

What Happens in Vegas ● ● ● ● ● ● ● ● ● ●

This film was directed by Tom Vaughan. Cameron Diaz and Ashton Kutcher star as two people who meet, get married quickly and then realise it was all a mistake. When they win $3 million, they each try to get all the money for themselves. It's meant to be funny, but I didn't laugh once. In the end, guess what? They discover they really love each other. It's so predictable!

Terminator Salvation ● ● ● ● ● ● ● ● ● ● ●

The Terminator machines have taken over the world and John Connor (actor Christian Bale) is the leader in the battle against them. I really wanted to see this because I'm a big fan of the earlier Terminator films. But I found it boring. The acting is wooden and the script is bad. People talk about the special effects, but to me they never look real and there's no excitement in the film.

Street Fighter ● ● ● ● ● ● ● ● ● ● ● ● ● ●

This 2009 film is based on a video game and it's set in Bangkok. Kristin Kreuk plays Chun-Li, a pianist and expert in martial arts, who goes out after a bad guy called Bison. It's a really silly story with awful acting. And there isn't even any good martial arts action! This is the worst film I've seen.

b Are the sentences *right* (✓), *wrong* (✗) or *doesn't say* (−)?

1 *What Happens in Vegas* is a romantic comedy. ☐

2 It cost a lot of money to make this film. ☐

3 *Terminator Salvation* is a science-fiction film. ☐

4 Christian Bale is a character who is played by John Connor. ☐

5 Robbie was disappointed by *Terminator Salvation*. ☐

6 *Street Fighter* was directed by Kristin Kreuk. ☐

7 Chun-Li was born in Bangkok. ☐

8 The film was made into a video game. ☐

c Have you seen the films in Robbie's blog? If so, do you agree with his opinions? Prepare to talk about this in your next class. Make notes to help you.

....

....

Portfolio 11

Write a review of a film that you <u>didn't</u> enjoy. Include the following:

• the director and the stars

• a little bit about the story

• your opinion

When giving your opinion, you might want to write about the story, the acting, the special effects, the setting or the music.

Quiz 11

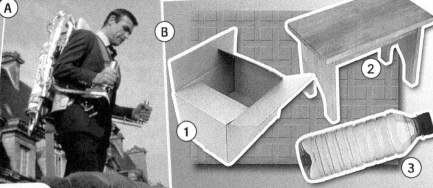

a What do you remember about Unit 11? Answer all the questions you can and then check in the Student's Book.

1 Match the words to make film people.

1 film ☐   **A** artist

2 camera ☐   **B** star

3 make-up ☐   **C** operator

2 Who is the famous film character in picture A?

He's _____ .

3 Circle the correct word.

Extras don't speak in films, so they don't need a *set / script / location.*

4 Choose the correct words: A, B or C.

Instructions are ¹_____ to the actors ²_____ the director.

1 **A** give   **B** gave   **C** given

2 **A** by   **B** for   **C** from

5 What was Ian Fleming's job?

_____

6 Complete the sentences with the verbs in the passive.

Today mobile phones _____ [use] everywhere, but they _____ [not invent] until the 1970s.

7 There are mistakes in these sentences. Write the correct sentences.

Were this book wrote by Philip Pullman? No, he didn't.

_____

_____

8 Name the materials for the objects in picture B.

1 _____   2 _____

3 _____

9 Can you find three words for materials in this puzzle?

r e b b u r r e h t a e l n o t t o c

_____   _____   _____

10 In which words is the *-ed* ending pronounced /ɪd/?

watched   reached   protected
produced   exploded

_____

b 🔊 74 Listen and check your answers.

c Now look at your Student's Book and write three more quiz questions for Unit 11.

Question: _____

_____

Answer: _____

Question: _____

_____

Answer: _____

Question: _____

_____

Answer: _____

12 Money talks

1 Vocabulary

Money

a Look at the table: 5 is S, 6 is R and 7 is E. Write all these letters in the puzzle. Then complete the money words and write the letters in the table.

1	2	3	4	5	6	7	8
				S	R	E	

9	10	11	12	13	14	15	16

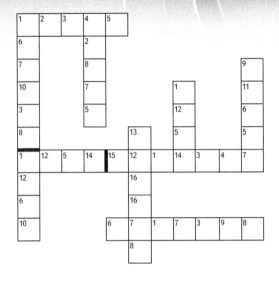

b Look at the pictures and complete the sentences with words in Exercise 1a.

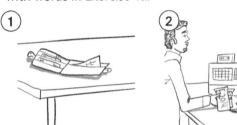

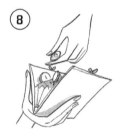

1 I've left my .... on the table.

2 He's giving the shop assistant two £20 ....

3 She's paying by ....

4 The shop assistant is giving him a ....

5 I'm going to use the ....

6 He's paying for the meal in ....

7 You need some .... for this machine.

8 She's putting the money in her ....

2 Grammar Grammar reference: page 94

Second conditional

a Match the two parts of the sentences.

1 If it was warmer today, ☐

2 I'd get a new computer if ☐

3 If I didn't enjoy playing basketball, ☐

4 I'd really miss my friends if ☐

5 I'd watch this channel more often if ☐

6 If these jeans weren't so expensive, ☐

A I'd buy them.

B they went away.

C I had enough money.

D I'd have lunch outside.

E I wouldn't do it.

F there weren't so many advertisements.

b Complete the sentences with the correct form of the verbs.

1 If I .... (be) older, I
   .... (ride) a motorbike.

2 I .... (learn) to ski if
   we .... (live) in the
   mountains.

3 If my parents .... (win) the
   lottery, they .... (buy) a
   new house.

4 Weekends .... (be) more
   fun if we .... (not get) so
   much homework.

5 If we .... (have) a
   swimming pool, I .... (go)
   for a swim every morning.

6 Dad .... (not feel) so tired
   if he .... (not have to)
   work on Saturdays.

c Complete the questions with the verbs in
the second conditional. Then write true
answers.

1 If someone .... (give) you 500
   euros, ... you ....
   (spend) it on clothes?

   ....

2 Where .... you ....
   (live) if you .... (can) choose any
   place in your country?

   ....

3 If you .... (know) a lot of
   famous people, who .... you
   .... (invite) to dinner?

   ....

4 If your home .... (be) on fire,
   which two things .... you
   .... (save) first?

   ....

5 How .... you ....
   (travel) if you .... (go) on a trip
   around the world?

   ....

③ Pronunciation

Long sentences

a Read the poem. Look at the endings of the lines
and (circle) the words that rhyme.

> If you were a singer, I'd buy all your records,
> If you were a model, you'd be a big star,
> If you made a film, it would win all the Oscars,
> You'd be a Ferrari if you were a car!
> If you were an athlete, you'd break every record,
> You'd jump seven metres and run like a dream,
> If you could play football, you'd be the top player,
> We'd win every match if you played in the team.
>
> Of course I'm just dreaming – it can't really happen,
> But if things were different, that's how they might be.
> And if I am lucky, when you read this poem
> It might make you smile and you might smile at me.

b 🔊75 Listen and repeat the first four lines after
the recording.

c 🔊76 Now practise saying the whole poem with
the recording.

Practise saying these words

🔊77 business   coin   company   millionaire
money   poor   private   purse   receipt
search   wallet   youth centre

---

④ Vocabulary

Money verbs

a Find seven more money
verbs in the puzzle. Write
them in the lists.

```
L  E  C  W  I  N  U
F  A  P  A  Y  B  R
E  R  O  S  T  O  S
G  N  I  T  A  R  P
S  A  V  E  N  R  E
W  R  L  A  B  O  N
I  L  E  N  D  W  D
```

Getting money: .win........................   ....

....

Keeping money: ....

Giving out money: ....

....

b 🔊 **78** Complete the conversations with the verbs from Exercise 4a. Then listen and check.

Ned: I've got four numbers in the Lotto! That means I'll ¹............................... about 500 euros.

Mum: Really? That's great! But listen, Ned, don't ²............................... it. Please use it for something sensible.

Dave: Are you going to the concert tonight?

Sam: No, I don't want to ³............................... any money this weekend. I'm trying to ⁴............................... money for a guitar. It's not easy!

Dave: Why don't you try to find some work? If you had a weekend job, you could ⁵............................... some extra money.

Aya: I'd like to get this, but I can't ⁶............................... for it. I've only got £10 here.

Elena: I can ⁷............................... you some money. How much do you need?

Aya: Could I ⁸............................... £12? I can give it back to you on Monday.

Elena: Yes, sure. That's fine.

Check it out!

The verb *pay* can be used with different objects. Look at these examples:

I paid for the tickets.
I paid £40 for the tickets.
I paid Helen for the tickets.
I paid Helen £40 for the tickets.

Help yourself!

Money idioms

Read these sentences. Then match the idioms (1–6) with the definitions (A–F).

- While he was a university student, he was **living on a shoestring**.
- We haven't got much money in the bank now. We'll have to **tighten our belts**.
- They've decided to buy a new sports car. They've got **money to burn**.
- They serve good food at that restaurant, but you **pay through the nose**.
- It's an awful job. We work long hours and we're **paid peanuts**.
- I'm going to **splash out on** a new dress for the New Year's Eve party.

1 live on a shoestring ☐
2 tighten your belt ☐
3 have money to burn ☐
4 pay through the nose ☐
5 be paid peanuts ☐
6 splash out on something ☐

A pay a price that is too high
B be very rich
C get very little money for your work
D spend more money than usual to buy something
E live on very little money
F spend less money than usual

Add the idioms to the list in your notebook. Include the example sentences, so you can see how the idioms are used.

5 Grammar Grammar reference: page 100

someone, anyone, everyone, no one, etc.

a Choose the correct answers: A, B or C.

Claudia: Has ¹.......... seen my sunglasses?
I can't find them ².......... .

Dad: They're probably in your bag.

Claudia: No, there's ³.......... in my bag.
I've taken ⁴.......... out.

Mum: Well, your glasses must be ⁵.......... ,
Claudia. ⁶.......... has taken them.

	A		**B**		**C**	
1	anyone		something		nobody	
2	anything		everywhere		anywhere	
3	no one		nothing		nowhere	
4	everything		everyone		everywhere	
5	nowhere		somewhere		everywhere	
6	Something		Nothing		Nobody	

b Use the table to make sentences.

1 I can hear someone at the door.
2 ....
  ....
3 ....
  ....
4 ....
  ....
5 ....
  ....
6 ....
  ....
7 ....
  ....

I can hear	anything	for his keys.
We aren't going	something	in my wallet.
Do we need to buy	nothing	~~at the door.~~
Sam has looked	anybody	next weekend.
I think	~~someone~~	on the phone last night.
I didn't speak to	anywhere	at the shops?
Oh dear! I've got	everywhere	is wrong with my watch.

6 Listen

a 🔊 **79** Listen to three people: Laura, Mark and Danny. Match them with the topic they are talking about. There are two extra topics.

1 Laura ☐   2 Mark ☐   3 Danny ☐

A a job   **D** a place to live
B a holiday   **E** watching films
C a present

b 🔊 **79** Listen again and find two things that are wrong in each picture. Write sentences with *would* or *wouldn't*.

1 She would live up in the hills.
  ....
2 ....
  ....
3 ....
  ....

⑦ Read

Read the blog. Then complete the sentences with the correct names.

---

sports forum — □ ⊡ ✕

http://www.sportsforum.co.uk/footballers

CRAZY money for footballers

Jess

12 July 11:25

I'm shocked at the money footballers are getting from the big clubs. Top players get more than £9 million a year (€10 million) – that's about £173,000 a week. These guys are earning over 300 times more than a police officer or a teacher. My mum's a nurse, she works incredibly hard and she helps to save people's lives – and she gets £21,000 a year! I think it's disgusting. Does anyone else agree?

5 comments

JohnK

12 July 16:10

It's sad, but that's how the world is. Millions of fans pay to watch football, but no one pays to watch a nurse working in a hospital. Everybody wants to see the best players and there aren't many of them, so their price goes up. That's business, Jess!

Beetle

12 July 20:04

If the money wasn't paid to the players, where would it go? To club directors and owners! But it's the players who have these incredible skills and they give us fantastic entertainment. Let them have the money and good luck to them.

Paula99

13 July 17:40

If players didn't get so much, clubs could give us cheaper tickets for matches. Yes, good players should earn good money, but the fans are important too. Lots of people can't go to see a match now because seats are so expensive.

Leatherman

13 July 18:35

Beetle is right. It's a free market and if that's what players can get, they should take it. We'd all take it too if someone offered it to us.

Chris

13 July 18:56

Why does everyone keep talking about football players? Racing drivers and golfers get more than footballers. And what about movie stars who can sometimes earn £30 million (€34 million) in one year?

---

1 .... and .... don't mind seeing footballers earn millions of pounds.

2 .... thinks that if footballers earned less, clubs could use the money for something else.

3 .... is angry about the money footballers earn.

4 .... doesn't give an opinion about payments to footballers.

5 .... thinks the situation is wrong but doesn't believe it can be changed.

6 .... shows that important jobs aren't well paid.

7 .... says that other sports people earn more money than footballers.

8 .... thinks everyone would be happy to earn millions if they could.

9 .... thinks that football fans have to pay too much money for tickets.

Portfolio 12

Add your message to Jess's blog, giving your opinion. Reply to at least two of the other messages in the blog.

- Make it clear which comment you are replying to.
- Give your opinion. (Do you agree or disagree?)
- Give reasons.

Quiz 12

a What do you remember about Unit 12? Answer all the questions you can and then check in the Student's Book.

A

B

Cool guys

Description	Amount
T-shirt	15.99
jeans	39.99
Total	55.98
Cash	55.98

C

ERID ALM
N
PS W

1 The man in picture A was on TV. What was the name of the show?

....

2 How old was Ben Way when he started his first business?

....

3 What can you see in picture B?

....

4 Are these sentences *right* (✓) or *wrong* (✗)?

a You can get coins from a cash machine. ☐

b People keep their credit cards in their wallet. ☐

c You need a PIN to pay for something in cash. ☐

5 Complete the sentence with the correct form of the verbs.

People .... (be) able to fly if they .... (have) wings.

b 🔊 80 Listen and check your answers.

c Now look at your Student's Book and write three more quiz questions for Unit 12.

6 Read this sentence and choose the correct meaning: A, B or C.

If we had a warmer climate, we'd be able to grow bananas.

A We can grow bananas now. ☐

B The climate was warmer in the past. ☐

C The climate isn't very warm. ☐

7 Write the question using the second conditional. Then complete the answer.

A: you / learn / to drive / if you / be / 17?

....

B: Yes, ...

8 Can you find four money verbs in the puzzle in C? Each word contains the letter *N*.

....

9 (Circle) the correct words.

We didn't see *something / anyone / somebody* on the beach, but there was rubbish *somewhere / anywhere / everywhere*.

10 There are two mistakes in this sentence. Write the correct sentence.

Everybody say there isn't nothing we can do about this problem.

....

....

Question: ....

....

Answer: ....

Question: ....

....

Answer: ....

Question: ....

....

Answer: ....

Grammar reference

1 Present simple and present continuous

Present simple

Positive			Negative			
I/You/We/They	**speak**	English.	I/You/We/They	**don't (do not)**	**speak**	English.
He/She/It	**speaks**		He/She/It	**doesn't (does not)**		
Yes/No questions				**Short answers**		
Do	I/you/we/they	**speak**	English?	Yes, I/you/we/they **do**. No, I/you/we/they **don't**.		
Does	he/she/it			Yes, he/she/it **does**. No, he/she/it **doesn't**.		
Information questions						
Where **do** you **work**? What subjects **do** they **study**? How **does** she **get** to school?						

- With *he/she/it*, the verb ends in -*s*.

  he walks   it moves   she watches   he carries

  ★ For the spelling of verbs with the -*s* ending, see Rules for spelling, page 100.

- We use *do/does* for questions and *don't/doesn't* for negatives.

- We use the present simple for permanent situations, regular or repeated actions, and facts.

  *Kelly **lives** in Berlin.   We always **play** basketball on Thursdays.*
  *Mike **doesn't eat** meat.   **Do** you **like** rap music?*

- We also use the present simple to describe events in a book or film.

  *In this film, Harry **returns** to his school and **receives** a mysterious book.*

Present continuous

Positive			Negative		
I	**'m (am)**	working.	I	**'m not (am not)**	working.
He/She/It	**'s (is)**		He/She/It	**isn't (is not)**	
You/We/They	**'re (are)**		You/We/They	**aren't (are not)**	
Yes/No questions			**Short answers**		
Am	I	working?	Yes, I **am**. No, I**'m not**.		
Is	he/she/it		Yes, he/she/it **is**. No, he/she/it **isn't**.		
Are	you/we/they		Yes, you/we/they **are**. No, you/we/they **aren't**.		
Information questions					
What **are** you **doing**? Where**'s** Helen **staying**? Why **are** they **laughing**?					

- For the present continuous we use *am/is/are* + verb + -*ing*.

  ★ For the spelling of -*ing* words, see Rules for spelling, page 100.

- We can also use these negative forms:

  *you**'re**/we**'re**/they**'re not** work**ing**   he**'s**/she**'s**/it**'s not** work**ing***

- We don't normally use the continuous form for these verbs:

  like love hate want need know think believe understand
  Do you need some help? (**not** ~~Are you needing~~)
  I don't believe that story. (**not** ~~I'm not believing~~)

  ★ For *taste*, *smell* and *sound* + adjective we also use the simple form, not the continuous.

  *Those flowers **smell** lovely.*
  *The sauce **doesn't taste** very nice.*

- We use the present continuous for actions happening now and for temporary actions.

  *Hey, look! It**'s snowing**!   Please be quiet. I**'m trying** to study.*
  *She **isn't working** today.   What **are** you **reading** at the moment?*

- We also use the present continuous to talk about future arrangements, often in the near future.

  *I**'m playing** tennis with Carlo tomorrow.   **Are** you **coming** to the party on Saturday?*

Grammar practice

1 Present simple and present continuous

a Choose the correct answer: A, B or C.

1 Somebody's phone is ....   A ring   B rings   C ringing
2 A lot of people .... waiting outside the cinema.   A is   B are   C don't
3 My parents .... speak Italian.   A isn't   B aren't   C don't
4 Liam .... watching his new DVD.   A is   B are   C does
5 Those actors often .... in television dramas.   A appear   B appears   C appearing
6 Anna .... take the bus to school.   A isn't   B doesn't   C don't

b (Circle) the correct words.

1 Mum isn't here right now. *She does / She's doing* the shopping.
2 David *wants / is wanting* to speak to you. *He calls / He's calling* from the station.
3 *I love / I'm loving* this film. *I think / I'm thinking* it's fantastic.
4 My brothers *play / are playing* rugby today. The team *practises / is practising* twice a week.
5 Kim is on holiday. *She spends / She's spending* ten days in Japan, but she *doesn't stay / isn't staying* in Tokyo.
6 *I don't understand / I'm not understanding* what this word *means / is meaning*.

c Complete the postcard with the verbs in the present simple or the present continuous.

Hi Louise
I ¹ .... (write) this at a campsite
near Grenoble. We often ² .... (come)
to France in the summer, but this year we
³ .... (not stay) in a hotel because
Dad ⁴ .... (not want) to spend a lot
of money. At the campsite I've met a boy called Karl. He's
Dutch, but he ⁵ .... (speak) English and
he ⁶ .... (teach) me to ride his mountain
bike. I ⁷ .... (have) a good time! I hope
you ⁸ .... (enjoy) your holiday too.

See you soon,
Petra

Louise Hamilton
52 Fitzroy Gardens
Dublin
Ireland

d Write the questions. Use the present simple or the present continuous.

1 A: you / watch / documentaries on TV?

   ....

   B: No, never.
2 A: Where / Gary / go?

   ....

   B: To the market. He wants to buy some shoes.
3 A: they / enjoy / their trip?

   ....

   B: Yes, I think they're having a good time.

4 A: How / Rosa / travel / to work?

   ....

   B: She catches the train.
5 A: it / rain / outside?

   ....

   B: No, not at the moment.

Grammar reference

② Past simple

Positive		Negative		
I/You/We/They/He/She/It	started. sang.	I/You/We/They/He/She/It	didn't (did not)	start. sing.
Yes/No questions		**Short answers**		
Did I/you/we/they/he/she/it	start? sing?	Yes, I/you/we/they/he/she/it **did**. No, I/you/we/they/he/she/it **didn't**.		
Information questions				
When **did** the concert **start**? Where **did** they **go** yesterday? What film **did** you **see**?				

● We use the past simple for completed actions in the past.
   *I **washed** my hair yesterday.   Raul **played** football last weekend.*
   *They **arrived** five minutes ago.*

   ✱ For the spelling of verbs with the *-ed* ending, see Rules for spelling, page 100.

● Regular verbs end in *-ed*.
   *jump → jump**ed**   like → lik**ed**   carry → carri**ed**   drop → dropp**ed***

● Many common verbs are irregular. They don't have the usual *-ed* ending.
   *speak → **spoke**   think → **thought**   fall → **fell**   go → **went***
   *They **flew** to Madrid on Tuesday.   Irena **bought** some books yesterday.*

   ✱ For a list of irregular verbs, see page 102.

● We always use *didn't* + infinitive for negatives and *did* + infinitive for questions.
   *We **didn't live** here ten years ago.   I **didn't speak** to Amy yesterday.*
   ***Did** you **enjoy** the film?   When **did** he **go** to London?*

③ *used to*

Positive			Negative		
I/You/We/They/He/She/It	used to	play.	I/You/We/They/He/She/It	didn't (did not) use to	play.
Yes/No questions			**Short answers**		
Did	I/you/we/they/he/she/it	use to	play?	Yes, I/you/we/they/he/she/it **did**. No, I/you/we/they/he/she/it **didn't**.	
Information questions					
What **did** people **use to do**? Where **did** we **use to play**? How often **did** she **use to visit**?					

● We use *used to / didn't use to* + infinitive for normal or repeated actions in the past. The actions don't happen now.
   *I **used to love** this music when I was about ten.*
   *At my first school we **didn't use to get** much homework.*
   *What **did** people **use to wear** in the 19th century?*

   ✱ Don't confuse *used to* + verb with the verb *use*.
   *I **used to take** a lot of photos.*
   *I **used** my phone to take these photos.*

Grammar practice

2 Past simple

a) Complete the tables of irregular verbs.

Verb	Past simple
1 ..see...............	saw
2	did
3	found
4	fell
5	knew
6	got
7	went

Verb	Past simple
take	8 ....
begin	9 ....
come	10 ....
wear	11 ....
sleep	12 ....
sell	13 ....
lose	14 ....

b) Complete the conversation with the verbs in the past simple.

buy   phone   be   talk   go   have   invite   do   meet   wear   not cost   not know

Ben: I ¹........................ a good time on Saturday.

Luke: Yeah? What ².............. you ....?

Ben: In the morning I ³.......................... shopping and I ⁴.......................... some new boots. They look great, and they ⁵.............................. a lot. Then in the afternoon Tony ⁶.......................... and he ⁷.......................... me to a party at his cousin's house.

Luke: Cool! ⁸.............. you .... your new boots?

Ben: Of course!

Luke: And how ⁹.......................... the party?

Ben: Well, at first I felt a bit lost because I ¹⁰.............................. many people. But then I ¹¹............................ this girl called Suzanne and we ¹².......................... for hours. It was really amazing.

3 used to

Complete the sentences. Use the verbs with the correct form of *used to*.

live   wear   ~~love~~   teach   not be   not travel

1 I used.to.love... playing with toy animals when I was a child.

2 People .... by plane in the 19th century.

3 .... your mother .... a uniform at school?

4 Mr Clark .... at our school, but he doesn't work there now.

5 Where .... you .... before you moved to this house?

6 There .... any shops in our village, but now we've got a supermarket and a chemist's.

Grammar reference

(4) Past continuous

Positive			Negative		
I/He/She/It	**was**	sleeping.	I/He/She/It	**wasn't (was not)**	sleeping.
You/We/They	**were**		You/We/They	**weren't (were not)**	
Yes/No questions			**Short answers**		
Was	I/he/she/it	sleeping?	Yes, I/he/she/it **was**.	No, I/he/she/it **wasn't**.	
Were	you/we/they		Yes, you/we/they **were**.	No, you/we/they **weren't**.	
Information questions					
Why **were** they **standing** outside? What **was** she **wearing**? Who **were** you **waiting** for?					

- For the past continuous we use *was/were* + verb + *-ing*.

- We use the past continuous for an action that was in progress over a period of time in the past.

  *It was a lovely morning. The sun **was shining** and the birds **were singing**.*
  *Sorry I didn't call you. I **was working** all morning.*
  *While Mum **was cooking**, we **were doing** our homework.*

- The past continuous often describes what was happening at a certain time. The action started before that time and continued after it.

  *At this time yesterday I **was sitting** on the beach.*
  *At 9:15 we **were** still **waiting** for the school bus.*
  ***Were** you **watching** TV at half past seven?*

> ✱ For the spelling of *-ing* words, see Rules for spelling, page 100.

(5) Past simple and past continuous

- We often use the past simple and past continuous together.
  *I **was cooking** the vegetables when Julie **arrived**.*
  *The accident **happened** while we **were driving** home.*

- We use the past continuous for a longer action. We use the past simple for a shorter action.

- The past continuous action started earlier. It was already in progress when the past simple action happened.

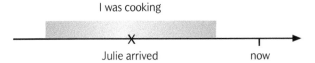

- The past simple action often interrupts the past continuous action.

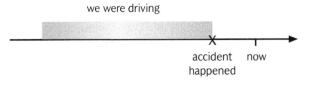

- We use *when* with the past simple and we normally use *while* with the past continuous. We can change the order of the two actions.

  While *they were having lunch*, | *the storm came* .   *The storm came* | **while** *they were having lunch*.

  When | *the storm came* , *they were having lunch*.   *They were having lunch* **when** | *the storm came* .

Grammar practice

4 Past continuous

a There is a mistake in each of these sentences. ~~Cross out~~ the wrong word(s) and write the correct word(s).

1 The sky was cloudy but it wasn't rain. ....
2 We was studying all day yesterday. ....
3 What they were carrying in those bags? ....
4 I couldn't read the menu because I wasn't wore my glasses. ....
5 Why Rachel were standing outside the library at 8:30? ....
6 On 1st August last year I stay in Prague for the summer holidays. ....

b Complete the sentences with the verbs in the past continuous.

1 Alex looked great. He .... (wear) black jeans and an orange shirt.
2 What .... Paula .... (do) at the police station?
3 At midnight the band was still playing and most people .... (dance).
4 We were worried about our cat because it .... (not eat) its food.
5 You were on the phone for ages! Who .... you .... (talk) to?
6 I saw them in town, but they .... (not ride) their bikes.

5 Past simple and past continuous

a (Circle) the correct words.

1 While we *cycled / were cycling* to school, it started to rain.
2 You *weren't / didn't* using the computer when I came home.
3 He *dropped / was dropping* his wallet while he *did / was doing* the shopping.
4 Sara *didn't take / wasn't taking* that photo while she *stayed / was staying* in Paris.
5 While I *made / was making* my bed this morning, I *found / was finding* my watch.
6 Jack *skated / was skating* when he *broke / was breaking* his wrist.

b Write the sentences. Use *when* or *while*.

1 I / study – Harry / call

....
....

2 He / find / some money – he / walk / home

....
....

3 We / wash up – we / hear / the news

....
....

4 I / see / you – you / play the piano

....
....

Grammar reference

6 Comparative and superlative adjectives

Adjective	Comparative	Superlative
quick	**quicker**	the **quickest**
safe	**safer**	the **safest**
fat	**fatter**	the **fattest**
heavy	**heavier**	the **heaviest**
honest	**more honest**	the **most honest**
intelligent	**more intelligent**	the **most intelligent**

Regular forms

● For one-syllable adjectives and adjectives ending in *-y*, we use *-er* for the comparative and *-est* for the superlative.

*In Europe, May is warm**er** than April.*
*The kitchen is the warm**est** room in our house.*

*It's sunn**ier** today than yesterday.*
*Tuesday was the sunn**iest** day last week.*

✱ For the spelling of *-er* and *-est* adjectives, see Rules for spelling, page 100.

● For most adjectives of two or more syllables, we use *more* for the comparative and *most* for the superlative.
*The Eiffel Tower is **more famous** than the Louvre.*
*He's the **most famous** actor in Hollywood.*
*Skateboarding is **more difficult** than riding a bike.*
*Maths is the **most difficult** subject for me.*

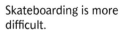

Skateboarding is more difficult.

Maths is the most difficult.

● When we use the comparative form to compare two things, we often use *than*.

● We normally use *the* with the superlative form.

Irregular forms

● Some adjectives are irregular in the comparative and superlative.

Adjective	Comparative	Superlative
good	**better**	the **best**
bad	**worse**	the **worst**
far	**further**	the **furthest**

*I'm quite good at singing, but Alice is **better**.*
*This is the **best** song they've ever recorded.*

7 Modifiers

Duck is	**much**	nicer	than chicken.
	a lot	tastier	
	a bit	more expensive	

● We can use *much*, *a lot* and *a bit* with comparative adjectives.

● We use *much* or *a lot* to express a big difference between things and we use *a bit* to express a small difference.

✱ We don't use these modifiers with superlative adjectives.

*Travelling by bus is **much** cheaper than flying.*
*Cats are **a lot** more independent than dogs.*
*The two rooms are almost exactly the same, but ours is **a bit** smaller.*

Grammar practice

6 Comparative and superlative adjectives

a Complete the table.

Adjective	Comparative adjective	Superlative adjective
1 poor	poorer	poorest
2 big		
3 funny		
4 strange		
5 disgusting		
6 good		
7 delicious		
8 hot		
9 lucky		
10 dangerous		

b Complete the sentences with the comparative or superlative form of the adjectives.

1 Martina's hair is .... (dark) and .... (curly) than mine.

2 He's one of the .... (popular) singers in the world.

3 The .... (luxurious) restaurants aren't always the .... (nice).

4 The armchair looks nice, but I think the sofa is .... (comfortable).

5 February was the .... (wet) month we've had for 20 years.

6 Their first album was awful and their second one was .... (bad)!

7 Modifiers

Complete the sentences. Use *a lot*, *much* or *a bit* with the correct form of the adjective.

1 My brother is ....
.... (old) than me.

2 The steak is ....
.... (expensive)
than the fish.

3 It's ....
(windy) today than yesterday.

4 This phone is ....
.... (cheap) than
it used to be.

5 The quiz show was boring. The
chat show was ....
.... (interesting).

6 The weather was ....
.... (bad) in the
afternoon.

Grammar reference

8 *will*

Positive			Negative		
I/He/She/It/ You/We/They	'll (will)	come.	I/He/She/It/ You/We/They	won't (will not)	come.
Yes/No questions			**Short answers**		
Will	I/he/she/it/ you/we/they	come?	Yes, I/he/she/it/you/we/they **will**. No, I/he/she/it/you/we/they **won't**.		
Information questions					
What time **will** they **get** here? Where **will** we **be** in ten years' time?					

- *Will* is a modal verb which refers to the future. The form *will* + infinitive is the same for all subjects.

- The negative form of *will* is *won't* (**not** ~~willn't~~). The question form is *will* + subject + infinitive.

> ✱ For other modals, see *might / might not* (below), *should/shouldn't* (page 86) and *must/mustn't* (page 88).

Predictions

- We use *will/won't* + infinitive to make predictions about the future.

  *In the future, tourists **will go** to the moon.*
  *He **won't want** to go camping in the rain.*
  ***Will** we **win** the match on Saturday?*

- We often use *think* with *will* predictions.

  *I think you**'ll enjoy** reading this book.*
  *I don't think it**'ll rain** tomorrow.*

Tourists will go to the moon.

Offers and spontaneous decisions

- We use *I'll* + infinitive to make offers.

  *I**'ll help** you with your homework.*
  *You must be hungry. I**'ll get** you some bread and cheese.*

- We also use *I'll / I won't* + infinitive for decisions that we make as we speak.

  *Tim isn't answering his phone. I**'ll send** him an email.*
  *I **won't go** out now. It's too cold.*

9 *might*

Positive		Negative	
I/He/She/It/ You/We/They	might change.	I/He/She/It/ You/We/They	might not change.

- Like *will*, *might* is a modal. It always goes with the infinitive of another verb, and its form doesn't change.

- The negative form of *might* is *might not*.

- It is possible to use the question form (*might* + subject + infinitive), but this is uncommon.

- We use *might / might not* + infinitive to say that something is possible but uncertain. It can refer to the present or the future.

  *Danny isn't in his room. He **might be** in the garden.*
  *It's only a small shop. They **might not sell** olives.*
  *We **might go** to the beach tomorrow, but it depends on the weather.*
  *I'll invite Sharon, but she **might not come**.*

Grammar practice

a Match the sentences.

1 Joel is working in Egypt at the moment. ☐
2 I haven't had a phone call from Sofia today. ☐
3 Leo hasn't trained for this race. ☐
4 There's something wrong with my speakers. ☐
5 Grace and Beth have missed the last bus. ☐
6 Adam isn't interested in history. ☐

A He won't win it.
B They'll have to take a taxi.
C We won't be able to listen to music.
D He won't want to go to the museum.
E I don't think he'll be home for Christmas.
F Perhaps she'll ring tomorrow.

b Choose the correct answer: A, B or C.

Greg: ¹............ able to finish our sculpture today?
Lee: Yes, ²............ . Mrs Anderson said we can use the art room at lunch time.

1 **A** We'll **B** We'll be **C** Will we be
2 **A** we'll **B** we will **C** it will

Alba: Do you think ³............ to university?
Juan: No, I ⁴............ think so. I'll ⁵............ to get into the computer design course at college.
Alba: That sounds interesting. ⁶............ enjoy that.

3 **A** to go **B** you'll go **C** will you go
4 **A** won't **B** don't **C** will
5 **A** try **B** trying **C** to try
6 **A** You **B** You'll **C** You won't

Dad: When ⁷............ here?
Amy: Well, the trains are running late, so I don't think ⁸............ before seven o'clock.
Dad: OK. ⁹............ cooking at about 6:30.
Amy: ¹⁰............ a lot to eat. We had a big lunch.

7 **A** Ellie gets **B** Ellie will get **C** will Ellie get
8 **A** she'll arrive **B** she arrives **C** she won't arrive
9 **A** I'll **B** I'll start **C** I started
10 **A** We need **B** We'll need **C** We won't need

Complete the sentences with *will/ 'll*, *won't*, *might* or *might not*.

1 Our new TV is arriving soon, but we don't know exactly when. It .... come on Thursday.
2 Tell your friends you'll be a bit late. I'm sure they .... mind waiting for ten minutes.
3 I'm not certain if Joe will come to the football match on Saturday. He .... go to the beach instead.
4 We can try the bookshop, but it .... be open. Some shops close early on Sundays.
5 It's so sad that Angela is moving to Canada! I .... really miss her.
6 I'm a bit worried about this present for Tim. He .... like it.

Grammar reference

10: *going to* for future plans

Positive				Negative			
I	'm (am)	going to	travel.	I	'm not (am not)	going to	travel.
He/She/It	's (is)			He/She/It	isn't (is not)		
You/We/They	're (are)			You/We/They	aren't (are not)		
Yes/No questions				**Short answers**			
Am	I	going to	travel?	Yes, I **am**.		No, I**'m not**.	
Is	he/she/it			Yes, he/she/it **is**.		No, he/she/it **isn't**.	
Are	you/we/they			Yes, you/we/they **are**.		No, you/we/they **aren't**.	
Information questions							
How **are** they **going to travel**? Where **is** he **going to meet** us? What **are** you **going to tell** them?							

- The form is the verb *be* + *going to* + infinitive.

- We can also use these negative forms:

  you**'re**/we**'re**/they**'re not going to** travel
  he**'s**/she**'s**/it**'s not going to** travel

- We use *am/is/are* + *going to* + infinitive to talk about future plans and intentions.

  I**'m going to invite** about 40 people to the party.
  Mum **is going to drive** us to the station at half past seven.
  We**'re not going to watch** TV tonight.
  When **are** you **going to see** the doctor?

> ✱ Future plans with *going to* are sometimes very similar to future arrangements with the present continuous. In some sentences both forms are correct.
>
> We**'re going to fly** to Rome on Monday.
> We**'re flying** to Rome on Monday.

11: *should* and *shouldn't*

Positive			Negative		
I/He/She/It/ You/We/They	should	leave.	I/He/She/It/ You/We/They	shouldn't (should not)	leave.
Yes/No questions			**Short answers**		
Should	I/he/she/it/ you/we/they	leave?	Yes, I/he/she/it/you/we/they **should**. No, I/he/she/it/you/we/they **shouldn't**.		
Information questions					
What **should** we **do**? How much medicine **should** I **take**? Who **should** she **talk** to?					

- *Should* is a modal verb. It always goes with the infinitive of another verb, and its form doesn't change.

- The negative form of *should* is *shouldn't*. The question form is *should* + subject + infinitive.

- We use *should/shouldn't* + infinitive to give advice. We use *should* if we think the action is a good idea. We use *shouldn't* if we think it isn't a good idea.

  You look tired. You **should go** to bed early tonight.
  She **shouldn't ride** her bike without a helmet.
  Should I **put** some more salt in this soup?

Grammar practice

10 *going to* for future plans

a Write a sentence for each picture.

		fly	some food
'm		study	the walls
's		do	the washing up
're	going to		
'm not		paint	to London
isn't		order	tennis
aren't		play	this evening

1 They ....

2 I ....

3 We ....

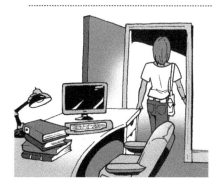

4 She ....

5 I ....

6 He ....

b There is a mistake in each of these sentences. ~~Cross out~~ the wrong word(s) and write the correct word(s).

1 I going to learn German next year.   ....

2 They're going opening the new swimming pool soon.   ....

3 Antonia isn't go to study this weekend.   ....

4 You going to wear your black dress tonight?   ....

5 We don't go to play basketball tomorrow.   ....

6 Does Paul going to look for a job in the summer?   ....

11 *should* and *shouldn't*

Complete the sentences. Use the verbs with *should* or *shouldn't*.

choose	talk	eat	look	spend	put

1 You .... so much time in front of the computer. Why don't you go for a walk?

2 We .... for a present for Ali. It's his birthday next week.

3 He .... all those chocolates. He'll get fat.

4 Both these jumpers are nice. Which one .... I .... ?

5 It's hot in here. We .... the milk in the fridge.

6 Anna's having problems at school. .... she .... to her teacher?

Grammar reference

12 *must* and *mustn't*

Positive			Negative		
I/He/She/It/ You/We/They	**must**	**leave**.	I/He/She/It/ You/We/They	**mustn't (must not)**	**leave**.

- *Must* is a modal verb. It always goes with the infinitive of another verb, and its form doesn't change.

- It is possible to use the question form (*must* + subject + infinitive), but this is not very common.

  > ✱ For questions, we normally use *have to*. See below.

- We use *must / must not* + infinitive for rules and obligations. We use *must* to say it is necessary or very important to do something. We use *mustn't* to say it is necessary or very important <u>not</u> to do something.

  > ✱ Don't confuse *mustn't* with *don't/doesn't have to*. See below.

  *Students **must follow** the school rules.*
  *Your exam was disappointing. You **must try** to work harder.*
  *Drivers **mustn't talk** on the phone while they're driving.*
  *I **mustn't forget** Dad's birthday on Sunday.*

- *Must/mustn't* can refer to the present or the future.

13 *have to* and *not have to*

Positive			Negative			
I/You/We/They	**have to**	work.	I/You/We/They	**don't (do not)**	**have to**	work.
He/She/It	**has to**		He/She/It	**doesn't (does not)**		
Yes/No questions				**Short answers**		
Do	I/you/we/ they	**have to**	**work**?	Yes, I/you/we/they **do**. No, I/you/we/they **don't**.		
Does	he/she/it			Yes, he/she/it **does**. No, he/she/it **doesn't**.		
Information questions						
What **do** we **have to do** for homework? Why **does** she **have to leave** so early?						

- We use *have/has to* + infinitive for actions that are necessary. Its meaning is similar to *must* + infinitive.

  *I **have to do** the shopping for Mum this afternoon.*
  *Michael always **has to leave** early to catch the 7:15 train.*
  ***Do** you **have to study** this evening?*

- We use *don't/doesn't have to* + infinitive for actions that aren't necessary.

  *Dad can relax at the weekend because he **doesn't have to work**.*
  *You **don't have to wear** a coat today. It isn't cold.*

- *Don't/doesn't have to* is different from *mustn't*.

  *You **mustn't** eat that.*   = Don't eat it!
  *You **don't have to** eat that.*   = It isn't necessary to eat it, but you can if you want to.

You mustn't eat that!   You don't have to eat that.

Grammar practice

12 *must* and *mustn't*

Complete the sentences. Use the verbs with *must* or *mustn't*.

tell	use	drive	remember	go	wear

1 I really .... to the hairdresser's. My hair looks awful now.
2 We're organising a party for Sonia, but it's going to be a surprise. You .... her about it.
3 The work is quite dangerous, so everyone .... a safety helmet.
4 I .... to get some money from the cash machine. I'll need it this evening.
5 We .... faster than 40 kph in town.
6 Passengers .... their phones while the plane is taking off.

13 *have to* and *not have to*

a Complete the sentences. Use the correct form of *have to*.

1 A: .... we .... (finish) this for homework?
   B: Yes, you ....
2 A: When .... you .... (leave)?
   B: In ten minutes. I .... (be) at the theatre before eight o'clock.
3 A: How far .... we .... (go)? This suitcase is heavy.
   B: But look, it's got wheels! You .... (carry) it.
4 A: Helen's lucky. She .... (wash) up or clean the house.
   B: .... she .... (help) with the cooking?
   A: No, she ....

b Circle the correct words.

We *mustn't / don't have to* pay!

I *mustn't / don't have to* go to school.

You *mustn't / don't have to* come in!

She *mustn't / doesn't have to* shout.

You *mustn't / don't have to* go on the road.

He *mustn't / doesn't have to* wear a school uniform.

Grammar reference

(14) Present perfect

Positive			Negative		
I/You/We/They	've (have)	**played** baseball. **written** a song.	I/You/We/They	haven't (have not)	**played** baseball. **written** a song.
He/She/It	's (has)		He/She/It	hasn't (has not)	
Yes/No questions			**Short answers**		
Have	I/you/we/they	**played** baseball? **written** a song?	Yes, I/you/we/they **have**. No, I/you/we/they **haven't**.		
Has	he/she/it		Yes, he/she/it **has**. No, he/she/it **hasn't**.		
Information questions					
What **have** you **done**? How many countries **has** she **visited**? How much money **have** we **spent**?					

- For the present perfect we use *have* + past participle.

- The past participle form of a verb is usually the same as the past simple.

   *She's **designed** some brilliant clothes.   He's **made** more than 30 films.   Have they **sold** many albums?*

   However, for some irregular verbs the past participle is different.

   *I've never **worn** a hat.* (**not** ~~wore~~)   *Have you **seen** this painting?* (**not** ~~saw~~)

   ✱ For a list of irregular verbs, see page 102.

- *Been* is the past participle of *be*, but it can also be the past participle of *go*. The verb *go* has two past participles: *gone* and *been*.

   *Cathy has **gone** to the gym.* (= She's still at the gym now.)
   *Cathy has **been** to the gym.* (= She was at the gym, but she isn't there now.)

Present perfect for experiences

- We use the present perfect to talk about actions at some time in the past up to now. We don't say exactly when they happened.

   *She**'s seen** this film three times this year.* (= from the start of this year up to now)
   *I **haven't tried** skydiving before.* (= at any time in my life up to now)
   ***Have** you **been** to Portugal?* (= at any time in your life up to now?)

Present perfect with *for* and *since*

- We also use the present perfect to talk about actions that started in the past and are still happening now.

   *I**'ve played** in this team for two months.* (I'm still playing in the team now.)
   *Dad **hasn't had** a holiday since April.* (He still isn't on holiday – he's still working now.)

- We use *for* + a period of time. We use *since* + a point in time when the action began.

   *Alex has been here **for two hours** / **since eleven o'clock**.*
   *I've known Lisa **for six weeks** / **since June**.*
   *We've had this car **for 12 years** / **since I was three years old**.*

Present perfect and past simple

- Past simple actions are finished – they belong to the past.

   *She **saw** the film three times last year.* (This happened last year – that time is finished.)
   *Alex **was** here for two hours.* (Then he went away – he isn't here now.)

- We use past time expressions (*yesterday, last week, in 2009, two years ago*, etc.) with the past simple but not with the present perfect.

   *I **didn't meet** your grandparents **yesterday**.*   *I**'ve** never **met** your grandparents.*
   ***Did** Kate **go** to Scotland **last summer**?*   ***Has** Kate ever **been** to Scotland?*
   *They **bought** their TV **a long time ago**.*   *They**'ve had** their TV for a long time.*

Grammar practice

14 Present perfect

a Complete the crossword with the past participles of the verbs.

Across	Down
3 take	**1** start
4 speak	**2** begin
6 sing	**4** study
7 buy	**5** know
8 do	
9 drive	

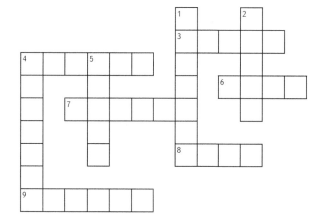

b Write the sentences. Use the present perfect and *for* or *since*.

1 We / have / this television / December

....

2 Nadia / be / at the sports centre / 4:30

....

3 I / not see / Simon / ages

....

4 They / know / my parents / 15 years

....

5 I / not play / this game / I was ten

....

6 your uncle / live / here / a long time?

....

c Choose the correct answer: A, B or C.

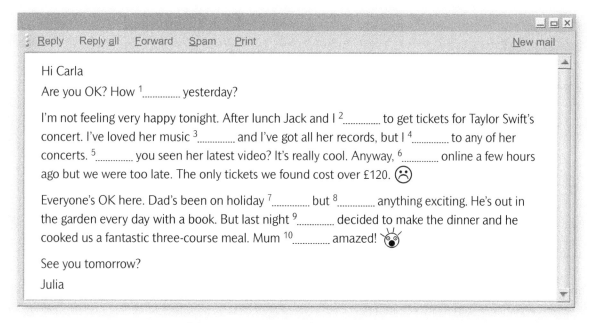

Reply   Reply all   Forward   Spam   Print   New mail

Hi Carla

Are you OK? How ¹............ yesterday?

I'm not feeling very happy tonight. After lunch Jack and I ²............ to get tickets for Taylor Swift's concert. I've loved her music ³............ and I've got all her records, but I ⁴............ to any of her concerts. ⁵............ you seen her latest video? It's really cool. Anyway, ⁶............ online a few hours ago but we were too late. The only tickets we found cost over £120. ☹

Everyone's OK here. Dad's been on holiday ⁷............ but ⁸............ anything exciting. He's out in the garden every day with a book. But last night ⁹............ decided to make the dinner and he cooked us a fantastic three-course meal. Mum ¹⁰............ amazed!

See you tomorrow?

Julia

1	**A**	was your exam	**B**	did your exam	**C**	has your exam been
2	**A**	has tried	**B**	have tried	**C**	tried
3	**A**	for years	**B**	since years	**C**	years ago
4	**A**	don't go	**B**	didn't go	**C**	haven't been
5	**A**	Are	**B**	Have	**C**	Did
6	**A**	we've gone	**B**	we went	**C**	we've been
7	**A**	for Friday	**B**	since Friday	**C**	last Friday
8	**A**	he didn't	**B**	he's done	**C**	he hasn't done
9	**A**	he	**B**	he's	**C**	he hasn't
10	**A**	was	**B**	have been	**C**	has been

Grammar reference

15 Zero conditional

Condition		Result
If	I **go** to the beach, plants **don't get** any water,	I always **take** my surfboard. they **die**.
	wood **is** wet, wood **is** wet,	it **doesn't burn** easily. does it **burn** easily?

Result		Condition
I always **take** my surfboard Plants **die** Wood **doesn't burn** easily **Does** wood **burn** easily	if	I **go** to the beach. they **don't get** any water. it**'s** wet. it**'s** wet?

- We use *if* when we want to show that one action depends on another.

- We use the zero conditional to talk about things that always happen in certain conditions.

- The verbs in both clauses are in the present simple.

- We can change the order of the two clauses. When the *if* clause comes first, we add a comma. When the result clause comes first, there is no comma.

They die if they don't get any water.

16 First conditional

Condition		Result
If	I **have** time, she **doesn't hurry**, it **rains** this afternoon, it **rains** this afternoon,	I**'ll (will) meet** you at the café. she**'ll (will) be** late. they **won't (will not) go** out. **will** they **go out**?

Result		Condition
I**'ll (will)** meet you at the café She**'ll (will) be** late They **won't (will not) go** out **Will** they **go out**	if	I **have** time. she **doesn't hurry**. it **rains** this afternoon. it **rains** this afternoon?

- We use the first conditional to talk about things that are possible in the future. The action depends on a condition that is possible but not certain.

  If I see Martin, I'll tell him to ring you. (Maybe I'll see him – it's possible.)

- In the *if* clause we use a present simple verb.

  *If I **see** Martin, …* (**not** *If I'll see Martin*)

- In the result clause, we use *will/won't* + infinitive.

- We can change the order of the two clauses.

Grammar practice

15 Zero conditional

a Match the two parts of the sentences.

1 If .... , the teachers get angry. ☐   **A** you put some salt on it

2 If you're online, ... ☐   **B** we don't do our homework

3 Food often tastes better if .... ☐   **C** there isn't anything interesting on TV

4 If .... , you get grey. ☐   **D** the grass doesn't grow

5 If it doesn't rain, ... ☐   **E** you can send and receive emails

6 I usually play computer games if .... ☐   **F** you mix black and white

b Write the sentences. Use *if* and the zero conditional.

1 I / not come / home early – my parents / start / to worry

....

2 our neighbours / have / a party – they / make / a lot of noise

....

3 this game / be / easy – everyone / follow / the rules

....

4 you / be / a shy person – you / not like / meeting new people

....

5 you / not can / be a good musician – you / not practise

....

6 people / live / in a tropical climate – they / not get / cold winters

....

16 First conditional

a There is a mistake in each of these sentences. ~~Cross out~~ the wrong word(s) and write the correct word(s).

1 The TV is sounding better if we get some new speakers. ....

2 If you'll catch the 7:30 bus, you won't be late. ....

3 If Diana doesn't find her wallet, she's very upset. ....

4 What we'll do if it rains on Sunday? ....

5 If James won't be here by eight o'clock, I'll leave without him. ....

6 If they'll drive from here to Manchester, how long will the trip take? ....

7 Antonio isn't able to play football next week if his finger is broken. ....

8 Emily comes to the party if we invite her? ....

b Use the correct form of the verbs to make first conditional sentences.

1 I .... (be) really disappointed if I .... (not pass) my exams.

2 If you .... (lend) me £5, I .... (pay) it back on Monday.

3 If the train .... (not stop) at Roseville, where .... we .... (get off)?

4 Pete .... (not make) new friends if he .... (not talk) to people.

5 If she .... (not be) careful, she .... (break) that glass.

6 What .... you .... (say) to Matt if he .... (phone) tonight?

Grammar reference

(17) Second conditional

Condition		Result
If	we **bought** a boat,	we **'d (would) sail** around the world.
	he **stopped** eating chocolate,	he **'d (would) lose** weight.
	they **didn't have** a map,	they **wouldn't (would not) find** this place.
	they **didn't have** a map,	**would** they **find** this place?

Result		Condition
We **'d (would) sail** around the world	**if**	we **bought** a boat.
He **'d (would) lose** weight		he **stopped** eating chocolate.
They **wouldn't (would not) find** this place		they **didn't have** a map.
Would they **find** this place		they **didn't have** a map?

- We use the second conditional to talk about unreal situations now or in the future. The action depends on a condition that is unlikely or impossible.

  *If I **had** wings, I**'d fly** to Australia.* (But I haven't got wings – this is impossible!)
  *Jill **would win** the race if she **practised** for it.* (But she probably won't practise, so this is unlikely.)

- In the *if* clause we use a past simple verb, but it refers to the present or future.

  *If I **had** wings, …* (**not** If I ~~have~~ wings or If I ~~'ll have~~ wings)

- In the result clause, we use *would/wouldn't* + infinitive.

- In the *if* clause we sometimes use *I/he/she/it **were*** instead of *was*. This is usual when the subject is *I*.

  *If I **were** you, I'd see a doctor.   If Lee **weren't** (or **wasn't**) so lazy, he'd be a brilliant student.*

(18) Question tags

Positive statement	Question tag	Negative statement	Question tag
<u>*be* present simple</u>			
I**'m** in the team,	**aren't** I?	I**'m not** a great singer,	**am** I?
We**'re** early,	**aren't** we?	We **aren't** ready,	**are** we?
He**'s** Polish,	**isn't** he?	She **isn't** from Italy,	**is** she?
<u>Other verb forms</u>			
You**'re** working,	**aren't** you?	You **aren't** listening,	**are** you?
He**'s** gone home,	**hasn't** he?	She **hasn't** left,	**has** she?
It**'ll** be fun,	**won't** it?	It **won't** rain,	**will** it?
They **can** fly,	**can't** they?	They **can't** see us,	**can** they?
I **should** leave,	**shouldn't** I?	I **shouldn't** be here,	**should** I?
You like olives,	**don't** you?	You **don't** eat meat,	**do** you?
She wears glasses,	**doesn't** she?	He **doesn't** drive,	**does** he?

- We use question tags to check information or to invite people to agree with us.

  *What's the time? I'm not late, **am I?**   It's a lovely day, **isn't it?**   This doesn't taste very nice, **does it?***

- We add a question tag to a statement. If the statement is positive, the question tag is negative. If the statement is negative, the question tag is positive.

- If the verb in the statement is *be*, we repeat the verb *be* in the question tag.

- For other verbs, we repeat the auxiliary or modal. (An auxiliary is a form of *be*, *do* or *have* which goes with the main verb. A modal is a word like *will*, *should* and *can*.)

- A positive statement in the present simple has no auxiliary or modal. Here we use *don't/doesn't* in the question tag.

Grammar practice

17 Second conditional

a Put the words in the correct order.

1 were / buy / cheaper / if / I'd / these shoes / they

    ....

2 had / we / watch / If / more time / we'd / that programme

    ....

3 some money / she / earn / She'd / a job / if / got

    ....

4 he'd / If / play / was / the basketball team / in / Mark / taller

    ....

5 come / you / would / everyone / you / If / couldn't / miss

    ....

6 were / eat / if / I / that fish / I / you / wouldn't

    ....

b Use the correct form of the verbs to make second conditional sentences.

1 If I .... (can) buy a motorbike, I .... (get) a Suzuki.

2 If it .... (not be) so cold, we .... (have) lunch outside.

3 My sister .... (be) a good actress if she .... (have) more self-confidence.

4 You .... (not arrive) late every morning if you .... (get up) earlier.

5 If we .... (live) near the beach, I .... (go) surfing every day.

6 How .... people .... (travel) if they .... (not have) cars?

18 Question tags

a Tick (✓) the sentence if the question tag is correct. If the question tag is wrong, ~~cross it out~~ and correct it.

1 It's really hot today, ~~is it?~~   isn't it? ....

2 He shouldn't do that, should he?   ....

3 They don't like Paula, does she?   ....

4 I'm in your class, aren't I?   ....

5 Peter can't swim, does he?   ....

6 We love this music, don't we?   ....

7 You'll be at the café, aren't you?   ....

8 Anna plays tennis, isn't she?   ....

b Complete the sentences with question tags.

1 We should visit Grandma this weekend, ... ?

2 They won't get here before ten o'clock, ... ?

3 I've got time for a shower, ... ?

4 You don't usually go to the market, ... ?

5 She hasn't been to Australia, ... ?

6 We'll finish this work this afternoon, ... ?

7 Dogs can't climb trees, ... ?

8 Adam plays the guitar in a rock band, ... ?

Grammar reference

19 Defining relative clauses

Main clause	Relative clause	
That's the boy	**who**	works in the newsagent's. I saw on the bus.
I've read the story	**which / that**	was in the school newspaper. you wrote.
We're in the street	**where**	Maria lives.

- A defining relative clause refers to someone or something earlier in the sentence. It gives essential information about the person, thing or place we are talking about.

- We use *who* for people. We can also sometimes use *that*.

  *I like <u>people</u> **who** make me laugh.*
  *My uncle is <u>an artist</u> **who** paints birds.*
  *<u>The teacher</u> **that** I like best is Mrs Harrison.*

- We use *which* or *that* for things.

  *He's wearing the <u>sunglasses</u> **which** he bought in Brazil.*
  *Has anyone seen <u>the magazine</u> **that** I was reading?*
  *<u>Buses</u> **that** go along Broad Street stop at the museum.*

- We use *where* for places. It means 'in which', 'at which' or 'to which'. There must be a noun or pronoun between *where* and the verb that follows.

  *We visited <u>all the places</u> **where** <u>they</u> filmed 'The Lord of the Rings'.*   (*where* = in which)
  *Barajas is <u>the airport</u> **where** <u>their plane</u> is landing.*   (*where* = at which)
  *That's <u>the restaurant</u> **where** <u>we</u> often go for a Chinese meal.*   (*where* = to which)

20 Verb + -ing and verb + infinitive

- The following verbs are followed by a verb + *-ing*:

  like   love   enjoy   hate   don't mind   finish   stop
  *He hates writ**ing** essays.   Have you finished clean**ing** your room?*

- The following verbs are followed by *to* + infinitive:

  want   need   hope   learn   agree
  *We need **to buy** some bread.   I hope **to work** as an architect one day.*

- The following verbs can take either form:

  start   begin   continue
  *It started **to rain** / **raining** at about ten o'clock.*
  *The plants will begin **to grow** / **growing** in the spring.*
  *She continued **to work** / **working** until midnight.*

> ✳ However, *like/love/hate + to + infinitive* is sometimes used, especially in US English.
> Also, remember that with **would** like (= want) we use *to* + infinitive.
> *I**'d** like **to see** that film.*
> ***Would** you like **to come** with us?*

> ✳ We can also use a noun or pronoun after most of the verbs in this section.
> *Have you finished that book?*
> *I need some new batteries.*
> *He hasn't started his essay.*

21 Infinitive of purpose and *for* + noun

- To explain why someone does something, we can use *to* + verb or *for* + noun.

  We're going to the café   **to have** lunch.
                              for lunch.

  She's gone out   **to get** some eggs.
                     for some eggs.

- We can also sometimes use *for* + verb + *-ing*.

  *These scissors are **for** cut**ting** paper.   A special camera is used **for** film**ing** underwater.*

Grammar practice

19 Defining relative clauses

a Use the table to make six sentences.

Nicole Kidman is	birds		they make sports equipment.
I haven't spent	to some tourists		can't fly.
Let's go	in a factory	who	was born in Australia.
Penguins are	an actress	which/that	were visiting our town.
My brother worked	to a café	where	you gave me.
We talked	the money		we can sit outside.

1 ....
2 ....
3 ....
4 ....
5 ....
6 ....

b Join the sentences. Use *who*, *which*, *that* or *where*.

1 She's a student. She was in my class last year.   *She's a student who was in my class last year.*
2 They've sold the shoes. I wanted to buy them.   ....
3 This is the house. My parents used to live there.   ....
4 They're recording a song. It was a hit in the 1960s.   ....
5 The man lives in Scotland. He bought our car.   ....
6 The town was really beautiful. We stayed there.   ....

20 Verb + *-ing* and verb + infinitive

Complete the conversation.

A: I want ¹.............................. (learn) ².............................. (cook) Japanese food.
I've started ³.............................. (collect) Asian recipes.

B: You really enjoy ⁴.............................. (work) in the kitchen, don't you?

A: Yes, I love ⁵.............................. (try) new dishes. When I finish
⁶.............................. (study), I'll try to get a job in a good restaurant.
I hope ⁷.............................. (be) a professional chef one day.

21 Infinitive of purpose and *for* + noun

Complete the sentences. Use these words with *to* or *for*.

get to the stadium   some money   a holiday   book her flight   Dad's 40th birthday   play baseball

1 I'd like to go to New Zealand ....
2 They've gone to the park ....
3 Sara is using the Internet ....
4 We're planning a big party ....
5 ...., you should take the 442 bus.
6 I need to stop at the bank ....

Grammar reference

22 Present simple passive

Positive				Negative			
It	's (is)	made	of metal.	It	isn't	made	of metal.
They	're (are)	written	in English.	They	aren't	written	in English.
Yes/No questions				**Short answers**			
Is	it	made	of metal?	Yes, it **is**.	No, it **isn't**.		
Are	they	written	in English?	Yes, they **are**.	No, they **aren't**.		
Information questions							
What **are** those tables **made** of? Where **is** Spanish **spoken**? How **is** this machine **used**?							

● Most sentences are active. The subject does the action.

Architects design buildings. (*Architects* is the subject and architects do the action of designing.)

In a passive sentence the subject doesn't do the action. It is the 'receiver' of the action, which is done by something/someone else.

Active: *Factory workers make these clothes in China.*
Passive: *These clothes **are made** in China.* (We don't say who makes the clothes.)
Active: *They give a prize to the best performer.*
Passive: *A prize **is given** to the best performer.* (We don't say who gives the prize.)

● We make the present passive with the present tense of *be* + past participle.

● We often use the passive when we don't know who/what does the action, or when it isn't important who/what does the action.

> ✱ For notes on the past participle form, see Present perfect, page 90.

● If we want to say who/what does the action, we use *by*.

*Buildings are designed **by** architects.*
*Safety equipment is worn **by** divers.*
*People are sometimes killed **by** snakes.*

23 Past simple passive

Positive				Negative			
It	was	invented	in the USA.	It	wasn't	invented	in the USA.
They	were	written	100 years ago.	They	weren't	written	100 years ago.
Yes/No questions				**Short answers**			
Was	it	invented	in the USA?	Yes, it **was**.	No, it **wasn't**.		
Were	they	written	100 years ago?	Yes, they **were**.	No, they **weren't**.		
Information questions							
When **was** the building **finished**? Where **were** they **born**? How **was** that scene **filmed**?							

● We make the past simple passive with the past tense of *be* + past participle.

*This umbrella **was left** on the bus.*
*Jeans **weren't worn** until the 19th century.*
***Was** the radio **invented** by Marconi?*

● When referring to the past, we use *be born* in the past passive form, not the present.

Michelangelo was born in 1475. (**not** ~~is born~~)

Grammar practice

22 Present simple passive

a There is a mistake in each of these sentences. ~~Cross out~~ the wrong word(s) and write the correct word(s).

1 This bag doesn't made of leather. ....
2 Sugar is produce in Jamaica. ....
3 Asian languages don't teach at our school. ....
4 What this gadget is used for? ....
5 T-shirts are often wore with jeans. ....
6 This track is sung from Leona Lewis. ....
7 Some unusual films are showed at this cinema. ....
8 In Japan tea not drank with milk. ....

b Use both boxes to complete the sentences. Use the present passive form of the verbs.

| Biscuits   A lot of pasta   ~~Rice~~   Oxygen tanks | use   ~~grow~~   speak   eat |
| French and German   The book | not write   not keep |

1 .Rice is grown.. in China.
2 .... in Italy.
3 .... in English.
4 .... for breathing underwater.
5 .... in the fridge.
6 .... at this hotel.

23 Past simple passive

a Complete the sentences with the verbs in the past passive.

1 Fantastic costumes .... (design) for the festival.
2 DVDs .... (not invent) until the 1990s.
3 The match .... (win) by Real Madrid.
4 Where .... these photos .... (take)?
5 The first movies .... (not film) in colour.
6 When .... the window .... (break)?

b Choose the correct answer: A, B or C.

1 The documentary was .... last night on Channel 4.
   A show   **B** showed   **C** shown
2 When .... that book written?
   A does   **B** is   **C** was
3 Potatoes .... in Europe before the 17th century.
   A weren't eaten   **B** aren't eating   **C** aren't eaten
4 Nobody .... us about the problem until it was too late.
   A told   **B** is told   **C** was told
5 Will Smith .... in 1968.
   A born   **B** was born   **C** is born
6   Our neighbours .... their house eight years ago.
   A bought   **B** was bought   **C** were bought
7 That's a nice bag. .... made in Italy?
   A Is it   **B** Was it   **C** It was
8 The artist .... a lot of her paintings to the museum in 1984.
   A gave   **B** were given   **C** was given

Grammar reference

(24) *someone, anyone, everyone, no one, etc.*

	some-	any-	every-	no-
People	someone	anyone	everyone	no one
	somebody	anybody	everybody	nobody
Things	something	anything	everything	nothing
Places	somewhere	anywhere	everywhere	nowhere

* We use these words to talk about people, things and places without saying exactly who/what they are.

* Words with *some-* refer to a particular person/thing/place that we can't identify. We normally use *some-* in positive sentences.

  ***Someone**'s taken my purse!*   *Let's have **something** to eat.*   *The information is **somewhere** on this website.*

* We often use words with *any-* in negative sentences and questions.

  *Hello? Is **anybody** there?*   *I don't want **anything** to drink.*   *Have you seen my keys **anywhere**?*

  We can also use *any-* in positive sentences when we want to say 'it doesn't matter which person/thing/place'.

  *This is easy. **Anybody** can do it.*   *I don't mind what we eat. Get **anything** you like.*
  *Put the boxes **anywhere**. I'll put them away later.*

* We use words with *every-* to mean all people/things/places.

  ***Everyone** needs food and water.*   *Is **everything** ready?*   *The park looks awful. There's rubbish **everywhere**.*

* Words with *no-* have a negative meaning. We always use them with positive verbs.

  ***Nobody** answered the phone.*   *We've got **nothing** in the fridge.*   *The room is full. There's **nowhere** to sit.*

* When a word with *some-*, *any-*, *every-* or *no-* is the subject of a verb, we use the singular form of the verb.

Rules for spelling

Verbs and nouns with -s

* Verb or noun ending in *-s*, *-sh*, *-ch*, *-x* and *-o*: add *-es*.

miss → miss**es**	bus → bus**es**
push → push**es**	dish → dish**es**
watch → watch**es**	lunch → lunch**es**
relax → relax**es**	box → box**es**
do → do**es**	hero → hero**es**

* Verb or noun ending in a consonant + *-y*: ~~y~~ + *-ies*.

carry → carr**ies**	ferry → ferr**ies**
fly → fl**ies**	comedy → comed**ies**

Verbs with -ed

* Verb ending in *-e*: add *-d*.

hate → hate**d**	invite → invite**d**

* One-syllable verb ending in a vowel + a consonant: double consonant + *-ed*.

stop → sto**pp**ed	grab → gra**bb**ed

* Verb ending in a consonant + *-y*: ~~y~~ + *-ied*.

hurry → hurr**ied**	study → stud**ied**

Verbs with -ing

* Verb ending in *-e*: ~~e~~ + *-ing*.

live → liv**ing**	come → com**ing**

* One-syllable verb ending in a vowel + a consonant: double consonant + *-ing*.

get → ge**tt**ing	shop → sho**pp**ing

* Verb ending in *-ie*: ~~ie~~ + *-ying*.

lie → l**ying**	die → d**ying**

* Verb ending in two consonants: add *-ing*.

  find → find**ing**

Adjectives with -er and -est

* Adjective ending in *-e*: add *-r* or *-st*.

nice → nice**r**, nice**st**	large → large**r**, large**st**

* Adjective ending in *-y*: ~~y~~ + *-ier* or *-iest*.

lazy → laz**ier**, laz**iest**	early → earl**ier**, earl**iest**

* One-syllable adjective ending in a vowel + a consonant: double consonant + *-er* or *-est*.

big → bi**gg**er, bi**gg**est	fat → fa**tt**er, fa**tt**est

Grammar practice

24 *someone*, *anyone*, *everyone*, *no one*, etc.

a Complete the words with *some*, *any*, *every* or *no*.

1 Are you doing ....thing tomorrow evening?

2 It's a good party, isn't it? ....body's enjoying it.

3 You've been great! Thanks for ....thing that you've done for us.

4 I can see Danny over there. He's talking to ....one on the phone.

5 This town is boring. There's ....thing to do and ....where to go!

6 I don't think ....body knows the answer to that question.

b Complete the conversations.

Greg: Where's James? I can't see him ¹................. .

Alex: He's not here and he isn't answering his phone. ²................. knows where he is.

Dad: Are you ready? Have you got ³................. ?

Julie: I'm just looking for my watch. I know it's here ⁴................. .

Dad: Well, hurry up. ⁵................. 's waiting for you.

Kate: It was really busy at the shopping centre. There were people ⁶................. .

Sam: Did you buy ⁷................. ?

Kate: No. I was hoping to get ⁸................. for Louise's birthday, but there was ⁹................. that I liked.

25 Rules for spelling

a Write the plural form of the nouns.

1 match ....

2 factory ....

3 helmet ....

4 body ....

5 glass ....

6 shop ....

7 monkey ....

8 baby ....

9 crash ....

b Write the *-ed* form of the verbs.

1 drop ....

2 dance ....

3 marry ....

4 jump ....

5 copy ....

6 taste ....

7 carry ....

8 offer ....

9 plan ....

c Write the *-ing* form of the verbs.

1 stand ....

2 give ....

3 stop ....

4 change ....

5 run ....

6 swim ....

7 die ....

8 put ....

9 breathe ....

d Write the comparative form of the adjectives.

1 happy ....

2 bright ....

3 fine ....

4 wet ....

5 crazy ....

6 big ....

7 safe ....

8 hot ....

9 clean ....

Irregular verbs

Verb	Past simple	Past participle	Verb	Past simple	Past participle
be	was/were	been	let	let	let
become	became	become	lose	lost	lost
begin	began	begun	make	made	made
blow	blew	blown	mean	meant	meant
break	broke	broken	meet	met	met
bring	brought	brought	pay	paid	paid
build	built	built	put	put	put
burn	burned/burnt	burned/burnt	read	read	read
buy	bought	bought	ride	rode	ridden
can	could	been able	ring	rang	rung
catch	caught	caught	run	ran	run
choose	chose	chosen	say	said	said
come	came	come	see	saw	seen
cost	cost	cost	sell	sold	sold
cut	cut	cut	send	sent	sent
do	did	done	set	set	set
draw	drew	drawn	shoot	shot	shot
drink	drank	drunk	shut	shut	shut
drive	drove	driven	sing	sang	sung
eat	ate	eaten	sit	sat	sat
fall	fell	fallen	sleep	slept	slept
feel	felt	felt	speak	spoke	spoken
fight	fought	fought	spell	spelled/spelt	spelled/spelt
find	found	found	spend	spent	spent
fly	flew	flown	spin	span/spun	spun
forget	forgot	forgotten	stand	stood	stood
get	got	got	steal	stole	stolen
give	gave	given	swim	swam	swum
go	went	gone/been	swing	swung	swung
grow	grew	grown	take	took	taken
have	had	had	teach	taught	taught
hear	heard	heard	tell	told	told
hit	hit	hit	think	thought	thought
hold	held	held	throw	threw	thrown
hurt	hurt	hurt	understand	understood	understood
keep	kept	kept	wake	woke	woken
know	knew	known	wear	wore	worn
learn	learned/learnt	learned/learnt	win	won	won
leave	left	left	write	wrote	written
lend	lent	lent			

Phonemic symbols

Consonant sounds

/b/  bird	/tʃ/  cheese	/d/  door	/f/ 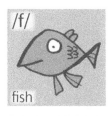 fish	/g/  girl	/h/  heart
/dʒ/  jam	/k/  key	/l/  leaf	/m/  monkey	/n/ 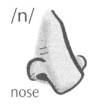 nose	/ŋ/ 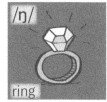 ring
/p/  pen	/r/ 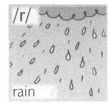 rain	/s/ 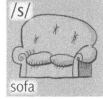 sofa	/ʃ/ 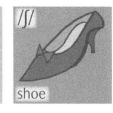 shoe	/ʒ/  television	/t/ 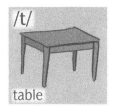 table
/ð/  feather	/θ/  think	/v/  volcano	/w/  window	/j/  yoga	/z/  zoo

Vowel sounds

/æ/  apple	/e/ 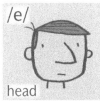 head	/i/ 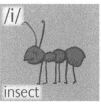 insect	/ɒ/  hot	/ʌ/ 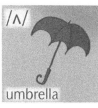 umbrella	/ʊ/  book
/ɑː/ arm	/ɜː/  earth	/iː/  sheep	/ɔː/ 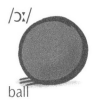 ball	/uː/  moon	/eə/  chair
/ɪə/ 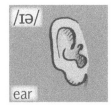 ear	/aɪ/ 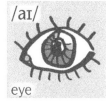 eye	/eɪ/  paper	/ɔɪ/  boy	/əʊ/  phone	/aʊ/  owl
/ə/  computer					

Go to the Interactive website to download the workbook audio.

www.cambridge.org/interactive